SEEDS

OF CONTINENTAL

UNITED STATES

LEGUMES

(FABACEAE)

Richard J. Delorit
Vice Chancellor and Professor of Agronomy
University of Wisconsin-River Falls
River Falls, Wisconsin 54022

Charles R. Gunn
Curator of the U.S. National Seed Herbarium and Botanist
Systematic Botany, Mycology, and Nematology Laboratory
United States Department of Agriculture
Agricultural Research Service
Beltsville, Maryland 20705

Printed in the United States of America
By F. A. Weber & Sons, Lithographers
Park Falls, Wisconsin 54552

Agronomy Publications
River Falls, Wisconsin 54022

Library of Congress Catalog Card Number: 86-71180

ISBN: 0-9616847-0-4

Preface

Accurate and rapid identification of species by means of seeds and fruits is important, especially for the seed technologist, agronomist, botanist, farmer, horticulturist, wildlife specialist, other scientists, and personnel of regulatory agencies. This book deals with seeds of the legume family, a major agricultural family, which also is one of the largest and most diverse plant families. The seeds and indehiscent one-seeded fruits, including loment segments and articles, are described and illustrated by color photographs. Environmental conditions and age may alter seed color, soil fertility and climate may affect seed or fruit size, and in some cases handling or harvesting may change seed or fruit sheen or damage some of the seed or fruit structures. Therefore, several seeds should be studied when making an identification.

The scientific names of some species have been changed in recent years. In these cases, the previously used names are listed as synonyms. Many species are known by one or more common names. Although long used, many of them are local names with limited use. Only the most widely used common names are included in this book.

We appreciate the comments and suggestions of *James A. Duke,* Research Leader, Plant Germplasm Laboratory, USDA/ARS, Beltsville, Md.; *Duane Isely,* Professor of Botany, Iowa State University, Ames, Ia.; *Joseph H. Kirkbride, Jr.,* Botanist, Systematic Botany, Mycology, and Nematology Laboratory, USDA/ARS, Beltsville, Md.; *James Lackey,* Staff Specialist (Botany), USDA/APHIS, Hyattsville, Md.; *Roger M. Polhill,* Assistant Keeper, Royal Botanic Gardens Herbarium, Kew, Richmond, England; and *Stephen Hurst,* Botanist, Federal Seed Laboratory, USDA/AMS, Beltsville, Md.

Table of Contents

The legume family has two scientific names recognized by The International Code of Botanical Nomenclature (Voss et al., 1983): Fabaceae (used in this book) and Leguminosae of authors including Isely and Polhill (1980). The family is divided into three subfamilies, Caesalpinioideae, Mimosoideae, and Faboideae and includes 650 genera and 18,000 species (Polhill and Raven, 1981; Gunn, 1983). Only the sunflower (Asteraceae) and orchid (Orchidaceae) families have more species.

The legume family is one of the two major agricultural families. The other is the grass (Poaceae) family. The agricultural value of legumes on a world basis has been documented by Duke (1981), Isely (1982), the National Academy of Sciences (1979), Skerman (1977), and Summerfield and Bunting (1980).

Legume plants store relatively large amounts of high quality protein in their leaves and seeds, making some valuable forage crops and also a concentrated protein source for both animals and humans. The protein derived from seeds of many species is especially valuable in developing countries, where the primary source of protein for humans is obtained from plant products. The most important legume food crops are soybean (*Glycine max*), peanut (*Arachis hypogaea*), beans (*Phaseolus* spp.), and pea (*Pisum sativum*), which account for about 90% of the world's legume production.

Legumes have a symbiotic relationship with certain nitrogen fixing bacteria (*Rhizobium*) in the soil. These bacteria, which help create and occupy nodules of the roots of legume plants, make atmospheric nitrogen available for plant growth. About three-fourths of the nitrogen used in the growth of the plant is derived from the atmosphere. The average amount of nitrogen fixed per hectare varies from 45 kilograms for beans and peanuts to 220 kilograms for alfalfa (*Medicago sativa*). From one-sixth to one-third of the nitrogen in legume plants is contained in the roots. Because nodulated legumes add substantial amounts of nitrogen to the soil, they are well adapted and widely used for green manuring and soil improvement.

Estimates of the number of legume genera and species in North America, including Greenland, varies from 114 to 136 genera and 1327 to 1523 species (Soil Conservation Service 1982 and Kartesz and Kartesz, 1980). This book recognizes 127 native and naturalized genera in continental United States, and 206 species were selected, primarily for their economic impact (crops, noxious weeds, trees, etc.) on U.S. agriculture. In addition to these genera, 14 other genera, listed in Appendix II, have been included to represent legume tribes and subtribes of the tribe Phaseoleae that are not native or naturalized in the United States. Thus all legume tribes and also the subtribes of Phaseoleae are included in this book. The distribution and origin of studied species was recorded from these recent floras and monographs: Barkley (1977), Barneby (1964, 1977), Correll and Johnston (1970), Fernald (1950), Gleason (1952), Hitchcock et al. (1961), Hulten (1968), Irwin and Barneby (1982), Isley (1973, 1975, 1981), Kearney and Peebles (1951), Long and Lakela (1971), Munz and Keck (1959), Radford et al. (1968), Scoggan (1978), Steyermark (1963).

The purposes of this book are twofold: (1) to illustrate by color photographs the seeds and one-seeded indehiscent fruits, loments, and articles of genera native and naturalized in continental United States and of at least one genus from each legume tribe and each subtribe of tribe Phaseoleae recognized by Polhill and Raven (1981) and (2) to expand the morphological data base for legume seeds, one-seeded indehiscent fruits, loments, and articles. One should not infer that the photographed seeds and fruits are typical or average representatives of the seed-fruit morphology of the genera they represent.

Procedures

Legume seeds and one-seeded indehiscent fruits used in preparing descriptions and photographs usually were selected from accessions in the U.S. National Seed Herbarium

(Gunn et al., 1977). A list of the source of seeds and fruits is deposited in the U.S. National Seed Herbarium.

Seed and fruit topographies were observed at 1 to 30 magnifications, using a dissecting steroscopic microscope equipped with an ocular micrometer.

Seeds were photographed, following a procedure established by Delorit (1970), on glass using a 35 mm Minolta SR T 101 camera, a bellows attachment, and KR 64 film. A 58 mm lens was used to photograph all except the largest seeds. They were photographed with a 135 mm lens. Magnifications varied from .22 to 2.4, depending on the size of the seeds. Lens openings of f/4 to f/8 were used for small seeds and f/8 to f/16 for large seeds. Light was provided by two fluorescent lamps equipped with cool white bulbs, and exposures of one-eighth to three seconds were used.

Except when limited by size or number of seeds available, photographs include eight or more complete seeds. The seeds were arranged in a manner which exhibits their most prominent characters, including the hilum. To position the larger seeds to show a selected feature, one or more seeds were glued to the glass. On the other hand, small seeds were cut with a razor blade to provide a stable surface. Because the appearance of seeds is affected by the color of background, seeds were photographed on different colored backgrounds, and the best combinations selected for publication. Special care was taken to obtain a balanced exposure for those species with light fruits and dark seeds.

Seed Morphology

Legume seeds possess a hilum (adnate to the seed coat); seed coat (testa), rarely absent; endosperm encasing embryo or adnate to the seed coat, or absent; and embryo with two well-developed cotyledons and a straight to bent or coiled embryonic axis. Seed characters support the concept of one family as advocated over the past 150 years, as well as the concept of three subfamilies: Caesalpinioideae, Mimosoideae, and Faboideae (Papilionoideae) (Gunn, 1981a, b). Both external and internal seed characters for the three subfamilies are illustrated in Figs. 1 and 2. For additional information about the legume seed coat, see articles by Lersten (1981) and Lersten and Gunn (1982).

Mature, dry seeds were studied, and their characters are discussed here in the same order as in the Catalog: Size, outline, compression, sheen, color, and surface topography; hilum shape, position, and visibility; presence or absence of collar, eye, colored raphe, and aril. In a few of the studied species, free seeds without a seed coat (it remains attached to the endocarp) do not exist in nature, i.e., angelin (*Andira inermis*) and psoralea (*Psoralea bituminosa*).

Size. Seed size is recorded in millimeters for length, width, and thickness and mostly as a range. Length is measured along the long axis of the seed without regard to hilum position. Width is measured at right angles and in the same plane as the length and at the widest point of the seed. Thickness, or short axis of the seed, is measured through the thickest part of the seed. Seed lengths range from 0.8 to 80 mm. At the low range are such temperate genera as *Lotus* and *Trifolium,* and at the upper range are such tropical genera as *Arachis, Caesalpinia, Dioclea, Entada* (the largest), and *Enterolobium.* Although most of the larger seeds are borne by woody tropical genera, two genera are herbaceous, *Arachis* and *Vicia.* Seed sizes of peanut (*Arachis hypogaea*) and broadbean (*Vicia faba*) have been increased through breeding and selection by man.

Outline. Seed outlines are categorized in sixteen shapes: Circular, cordate, C-shaped, D-shaped, elliptic, falcate, irregular, mitten shaped, oblong, ovate, rectangular, reniform, rhomboid, square, trapeziform, triangular, or modifications of these shapes including dents or notches.

Transection. Seed transections are arbitrarily categorized as terete with a 1:1 ratio, compressed with more or less a 2:1 ratio, and flattened with more than a 4:1 ratio. The separation between compressed and terete is arbitrary, because there is no distinct break between the 2:1 and 1:1 ratios.

Sheen. Legume seed coats usually are thought to be glossy but this survey, like others, demonstrates that sheen ranges from glossy to semiglossy and dull. Occasionally sheen may be modified by a bloom (lentil, *Lens culinaris*), a fruit exudate (purple lonchocarpus, *Lonchocarpus violaceus*), or adnation of endocarp tissue (wild-bean, *Strophostyles helvola*).

Color. Seed coats usually are light to dark brown or a brown derivative: Buff, ivory, ochre, or tan. Less frequent colors are black, gray, green, purple, red (including rosy and scarlet), white, and yellow, or derivations of these colors. In most genera the seeds are monochrome and this fact is not recorded. Some of the studied genera have mottled or streaked seeds, and a few genera have bichrome seed coats with two distinct areas of different colors. Both states are recorded and in either case the colors are the same as those listed above.

Surface topography. Seed coat surfaces are usually clearly visible, except for a few species, such as the West Indian-locust (*Hymenaea courbaril*) or wild-bean, whose seed coats are partially or completely concealed by adnate endocarp tissue. Seed coats at low magnifications of 10 or less may be smooth or ornamented. Ornamentation includes areole, fracture lines (concentric or reticulate), fruit exudates, grooves, indentations, pits, pleurograms, pseudopleurograms, raised cuticular patches, ridges, striations, tubercules, and wrinkles (rugose).

Fracture lines are formed during seed maturation and are thought to be the results of seed shrinkage during the internal drying process. They are cracks in the cuticle, which is a waxy or fatty coat that covers the testa and is relatively impermeable to water. Isely (1955) described fracture lines as "contiguous, curving lines of translucent cracks . . . and more or less obscuring the cellular surface beneath." This network of fracture lines is not found on the faces of faboid seeds. A few faboid seeds have fracture lines adjacent to the hilum. Faboid seeds usually have a thinner cuticle than most mimosoid and caesalpinioid seeds. The relationship of fracture line formation to cuticle thickness has not been established. Some of the seeds with the thickest cuticles do not have fracture lines. Fracture lines are present on the faces of seeds in 30 percent of the mimosoid genera and 26 percent of the caesalpinioid genera.

Most seed coat pits are superficial indentations. The pits in the seed coats of some *Bauhinia* spp. (Rugenstein and Lersten, 1981) as well as the desert-ironwood (*Olneya tesota*) are stomata.

Pleurograms (and pseudopleurograms) are rare in seed-bearing plant families, occurring only in the legume and cucumber (Curcurbitaceae) families. Corner (1976) noted that "most modifications of the ovule in the course of its development into the seed affect the hilum, the chalaza (lens), or the periphery." Few affect the faces or lateral sides of seeds, and these are pleurograms (face lines of Isely, 1955; light lines from the early 19th century; linea fissura of Boelcke, 1946; and linea sutura of Capitaine, 1912). Pleurograms always are present in 31 genera and absent or present in 8 genera of the 62-genus subfamily Mimosoideae, pleurograms or pseudopleurograms are present in six genera and absent or present in two genera of the 152-genus subfamily Caesalpinioideae. Both are absent in the 442-genus subfamily Faboideae. The pleurogram is a gaping break in the exotestal palisades, and it has a uniform origin and usually a uniform shape. The pleurogram may be close to the margin (never along the margin) or interior and small in relationship to seed length and width. Statements have been made to the effect that mimosoid pleurograms function as a hygroscopic valve. There is no documentation of this theory. However, during imbibition, the seed coat often separates along the pleurogram. The area encompassed by the pleurogram is labeled the areole and usually has the same surface texture as the seed coat outside the pleurogram. Occasionally the texture of the areole may have subtle to distinct differences when com-

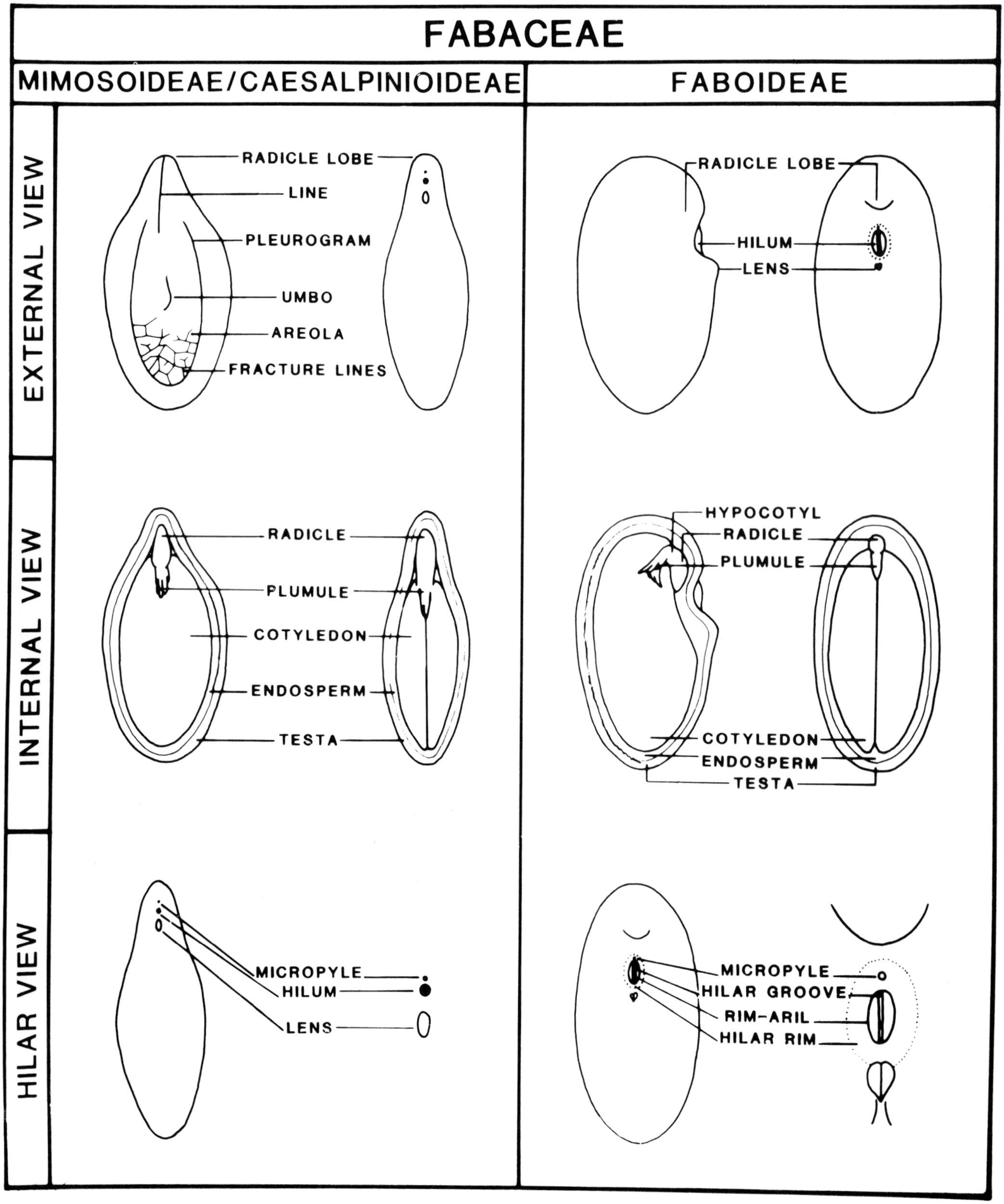

FABACEAE

MIMOSOIDEAE/CAESALPINIOIDEAE	FABOIDEAE

EXTERNAL VIEW

- RADICLE LOBE
- LINE
- PLEUROGRAM
- UMBO
- AREOLA
- FRACTURE LINES

- RADICLE LOBE
- HILUM
- LENS

INTERNAL VIEW

- RADICLE
- PLUMULE
- COTYLEDON
- ENDOSPERM
- TESTA

- HYPOCOTYL
- RADICLE
- PLUMULE
- COTYLEDON
- ENDOSPERM
- TESTA

HILAR VIEW

- MICROPYLE
- HILUM
- LENS

- MICROPYLE
- HILAR GROOVE
- RIM-ARIL
- HILAR RIM

Fabaceae Seed Terminology

PLEUROGRAM

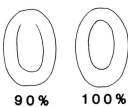

90%   100%

EYE

COLLAR

RIM-ARIL

TONGUE-ARIL

Fabaceae Fruit Terminology

LEGUME

FOLLICLE

SEED

LOMENT

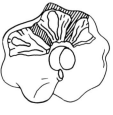

SEED

ARTICLE

FRUIT   ARTICLE   SEED IN SITU

pared to the seed coat on the outside of the pleurogram. The pseudopleurogram in the genera of subfamily Caesalpinioideae included in this book is a colored line in the exotestal palisades, and not a break in this layer.

Hilum. The hilum is the scar where the funicule joined the seed coat. The mimosoid and caesalpinioid hila are simple and unspecialized structures and are usually described as small or punctiform and, even with collateral hilar characters, have little diagnostic value. There is no tracheid bar, hilar split, or rim-aril that usually are found associated with the faboid hilum. These hila, often with collateral characters, have diagnostic value.

Shapes. Hilum shapes are categorized in eight shapes: Circular, elliptic, linear, oblong, ovate, punctiform, V-shaped, and wedge-shaped. The circular and punctiform shapes are the same. The difference is one of diameter: Circular is 1 mm or more in diameter, and punctiform is less than 1 mm in diameter. A linear hilum has at least a 1:10 length-width ratio.

Position. Hilum positions range from apical to subapical or marginal. The hilum positions are either apical or subapical for genera in subfamilies Mimosoideae or Caesalpiniodeae, except *Bauhinia* where it is marginal. Most faboid seeds have a marginal hilum.

Visibility. The hilum may be exposed or partially concealed by a funicular remnant or completely concealed by a funicule or aril. If hilar visibility is not recorded, the hilum is exposed.

Collar and eye. A few hila of faboid genera may be surrounded by a raised collar, not an aril, which may be the same color as the seed coat, lighter or darker, or another color. If another color, the collar also may be known as an eye or a halo. This eye may be a colored band around the hilum, not a raised area.

Colored raphe. The raphe may be traced between the hilum and the base of the seed and may be the color of the seed coat or not and may be a ridge or not. Only the most conspicuous colored raphes are noted.

Aril. The fleshy aril is an enlarged hardened funicule and of fruit origin, though adnate to the free seed. Some of the most elaborate arils are found in the introduced Australian species of *Acacia,* and less conspicuous fleshy arils are found on seeds like those of Texas brongniarta (*Brongniartia minutiflora*). In addition to the fleshy arils which cover the hilum, there also are dry arils, the rim-aril and tongue-aril (Fig. 2). These dry arils are frequently found on seeds from species of tribe Phaseoleae.

Fruit and Calyx Morphology

The legume fruit, which has several forms illustrated in Fig. 2, is a fertilized mature ovary. Fruits may be dehiscent (opening regularly exposing one or more mature seeds) or may be indehiscent (remaining closed around one or more mature seeds). Dehiscent fruits of the legume family are known as 'legumes.' These dry legumes usually dehisce violently under helicoidal bending of the valves and propel seeds away from the fruit. On the other hand, some legumes open passively along both sutures like a pair of scissors or along one suture like a follicle. Legumes and the following fruit types usually are three-layered: Epicarp (outer layer), mesocarp (middle layer, which may be fibrous and spongy or not), and endocarp (inner layer next to the seeds). Because the legume dehisces, it is beyond the scope of this study. The one-seeded indehiscent fruits and fruit segments (loments or articles) are described and photographed, because these are units of dissemination. Loments are specialized multiseeded legume fruits that break into transverse one-seeded indehiscent segments. Articles are lomentlike endocarp segments that fall free of the mesocarp and epicarp. Hog-peanut (*Amphicarpaea bracteata*), which is the only studied species to produce more than one type of fruit, produces three fruit types.

Mature, dry one-seeded indehiscent fruits, loments, and articles were studied, and their characters are discussed here in the same order as in the Catalog: Type of fruit, calyx characters if fruit concealed by calyx, size, outline, compression, sheen, color, surface topography, and calyx characters if calyx not concealing fruit. When appropriate, these characters are illustrated in Fig. 2.

Type of fruit. One-seeded indehiscent fruits, loment segments, and articles were studied.

Size. Fruit, loment, or article sizes are recorded in millimeters for length, width, and thickness and mostly as a range. Length is measured along the long axis and width at right angles and in the same plane as length and at the widest part. Thickness, or short axis of the fruit, is measured through the thickest point. Five of six longest (20 mm or more in length) one-seeded indehiscent fruits are tropical woody species: Tonka-bean, *Dipteryx odorata;* pongam, *Pongamia pinnata;* dalbergia, *Dalbergia sissoo;* angelin, *Andira inermis;* and logwood, *Haematoxylum campechianum.* The next largest fruit is from the herbaceous crop, peanut (*Arachis hypogaea*). The three longest (10 mm or more in length) loment segments and articles are of temperate origin (mesquite, *Prosopis glandulosa;* sweet-vetch, *Hedysarum alpinum* var. *americanum;* and tick-trefoil, *Desmodium glutinosum*).

Outline. Outlines are categorized in fourteen shapes: Circular, C-shaped, D-shaped, elliptic, falcate, fusiform, lanceolate, mitten shaped, oblong, obovate, ovate, rhombic, square, and triangular.

Transection. Fruit transections are arbitrarily categorized as terete with a 1:1 ratio, compressed with more or less a 2:1 ratio, and flattened with more than a 4:1 ratio. The separation between compressed and terete is arbitrary, because there is no distinct break between the 2:1 and 1:1 ratios.

Sheen. Only one studied fruit is semiglossy (white clover, *Trifolium repens*); the others were dull.

Color. Most studied fruits are light brown to brown or a brown derivative: Buff, ochre, golden, or tan. Less frequent colors are black, gray, green, yellow, or derivations of these colors.

Surface topography. Surfaces at low magnifications of 10 or less may be ornamented or smooth. Ornamentation includes glands, hairs (straight or with hooked apices), honeycombed, lined, reticulated, ribbed, rugose surfaces, or spines, spiny crests, and tubercles.

One-seeded indehiscent fruits may or may not have an indurate calyx. When present, the calyx may partially or completely conceal the fruit. When the fruit is concealed, the calyx presence and topography are recorded before the fruit size, and when the fruit is partially concealed, the calyx presence and topography are recorded at the end of the fruit description.

Guides to Seed Characters

These guides are a series of key character statements that were selected from the seed descriptions to facilitate locating genera in the Catalog. Some of the terms used in the Guides and in the Catalog are illustrated in Figs. 1 and 2. The guide data sequence is the same as in the text in the Catalog. Only those characters that are shared by 20 genera or less are listed. The listing of a genus name within a guide connotes that at least one species in the genus exhibits the listed character.

The numbers assigned to the genera can be used as an aid in identification by first selecting the most obvious character of the seed being identified and writing down the numbers of the genera listed under that character. Another seed character should then be selected and the numbers of the genera not appearing under this character crossed off the original list. This process should be repeated until the number of choices has been significantly reduced.

SEED WITH THIN TESTA OR WITHOUT TESTA
12 *Andira* (thin testa)
15 *Arachis* (thin testa)
117 *Psoralea* (testa absent)

SEED LENGTH

UP TO 2 MM LONG

9 *Alysicarpus*
16 *Astragalus*
45 *Dalea*
74 *Indigofera*
80 *Lespedeza*
83 *Lotus*
88 *Marina*
89 *Medicago*
90 *Melilotus*
101 *Ornithopus*
102 *Oxytropis*
136 *Trifolium*
139 *Vicia*

20 MM OR MORE LONG

15 *Arachis*
21 *Caesalpinia*
24 *Canavalia*
47 *Delonix*
51 *Dioclea*
53 *Dipteryx*
54 *Entada*
55 *Enterolobium*
72 *Hymenaea*
93 *Mucuna*
109 *Phaseolus*
115 *Pongamia*
132 *Swartzia*
139 *Vicia*

SEED SHAPE

CORDATE

21 *Caesalpinia*
54 *Entada*

C-SHAPED

5 *Aeschynomene*
49 *Desmodium*
82 *Lonchocarpus*
89 *Medicago*
97 *Onobrychis*
109 *Phaseolus*
123 *Scorpiurus*

D-SHAPED

4 *Adesmia*
5 *Aeschynomene*

D-SHAPED (Cont.)

49 *Desmodium*
89 *Medicago*
100 *Orbexilum*

FALCATE

17 *Baptisia*
49 *Desmodium*
59 *Eysenhardtia*
86 *Maackia*
95 *Nissolia*
106 *Parryella*
118 *Psorothamnus*
121 *Robinia*
131 *Stylosanthes*
142 *Zornia*

MITTEN SHAPED
16 *Astragalus*
26 *Carmichaelia*
37 *Colutea*
41 *Crotalaria*
43 *Cytisus*
45 *Dalea*
83 *Lotus*
88 *Marina*
90 *Melilotus*
98 *Ononis*
102 *Oxytropis*
128 *Sphaerophysa*
136 *Trifolium*
138 *Ulex*

RECTANGULAR
28 *Centrosema*
31 *Chamaecrista*
137 *Trigonella*
139 *Vicia*
140 *Vigna*

RENIFORM
35 *Clitoria*

RHOMBOID
124 *Senna*

SQUARE
31 *Chamaecrista*
40 *Cracca*
42 *Cyamopsis*
74 *Indigofera*
78 *Lathyrus*
84 *Lupinus*
127 *Spartium*
129 *Sphinctospermum*

TRAPEZOID
92 *Mimozyganthus*
137 *Trigonella*

TRIANGULAR
21 *Caesalpinia*
89 *Medicago*
139 *Vicia*

SEED TRANSECTION: FLATTENED
2 *Acacia*
21 *Caesalpinia*
44 *Dalbergia*
48 *Desmanthus*
49 *Desmodium*
64 *Gleditsia*
69 *Haematoxylum*
70 *Hedysarum*
92 *Mimozyganthus*
107 *Peltophorum*

SEED SHEEN: CONCEALED BY BLOOM, EXUDATE, OR ENDOCARP
72 *Hymenaea* (partially or completely concealed by endocarp tissue)
79 *Lens* (gray bloom)
82 *Lonchocarpus* (often with glossy fruit exudate)
130 *Strophostyles* (partially or completely concealed by endocarp tissue)
134 *Tephrosia* (partially concealed by whitish endocarp tissue)
139 *Vicia* (gray bloom)

SEED COLOR

BLACK
  1 *Abrus*
  6 *Afzelia*
 11 *Amphicarpaea*
 16 *Astragalus*
 33 *Cicer*
 46 *Daviesia*
 51 *Dioclea*
 58 *Euchresta*
 59 *Eysenhardtia*
 66 *Glycine*
 89 *Medicago*
 93 *Mucuna*
109 *Phaseolus*
110 *Pickeringia*
111 *Piscidia*
113 *Pithecellobium*
139 *Vicia*
140 *Vigna*

BUFF/IVORY/WHITE
 15 *Arachis*
 24 *Canavalia*
 33 *Cicer*
 38 *Coronilla*
 66 *Glycine*
 89 *Medicago*
 93 *Mucuna*
109 *Phaseolus*

BUFF/IVORY/WHITE
120 *Rhynchosia*
136 *Trifolium*
139 *Vicia*

GRAY
  2 *Acacia*
 21 *Caesalpinia*
 79 *Lens*
 84 *Lupinus*

GREEN
 33 *Cicer*
 89 *Medicago*
138 *Ulex*
139 *Vicia*

PURPLE
 15 *Arachis*
136 *Trifolium*
139 *Vicia*
140 *Vigna*

RED/SCARLET
  1 *Abrus*
  3 *Adenanthera*
 15 *Arachis*
 57 *Erythrina*

SEED SURFACE

FRACTURE LINES
  2 *Acacia*
  3 *Adenanthera*
  7 *Albizia*
 21 *Caesalpinia*
 29 *Ceratonia*
 31 *Chamaecrista*
 47 *Delonix*
 54 *Entada*
 64 *Gleditsia*
 68 *Gymnocladus*
 81 *Leucaena*
 85 *Lysiloma*
 91 *Mimosa*
 94 *Neptunia*
105 *Parkinsonia*
107 *Peltophorum*
116 *Prosopis*
124 *Senna*
133 *Tamarindus*

PLEUROGRAM AND
PSEUDOPLEUROGRAM
  2 *Acacia*
  3 *Adenanthera*
  7 *Albizia*
 23 *Calliandra*
 48 *Desmanthus*
 50 *Dichrostachys*
 55 *Enterolobium*
 81 *Leucaena*
 85 *Lysiloma*
 91 *Mimosa*
 94 *Neptunia*
104 *Parkia*
113 *Pithecellobium*
116 *Prosopis*
122 *Schrankia*
124 *Senna*
133 *Tamarindus*

HILUM SHAPE

CIRCUMLINEAR
- 51 *Dioclea*
- 93 *Mucuna*
- 139 *Vicia*

ELLIPTIC
- 1 *Abrus*
- 42 *Cyamopsis*
- 52 *Diphysa*
- 57 *Erythrina*
- 84 *Lupinus*
- 86 *Maackia*
- 103 *Pachyrrhizus*
- 112 *Pisum*
- 117 *Psoralea*
- 139 *Vicia*

LINEAR
- 18 *Bauhinia*
- 51 *Dioclea*
- 76 *Lablab*
- 78 *Lathyrus*
- 79 *Lens*
- 93 *Mucuna*

LINEAR (Cont.)
- 130 *Strophostyles*
- 139 *Vicia*
- 140 *Vigna*

OBLONG
- 41 *Crotalaria*
- 60 *Galactia*
- 65 *Glottidium*
- 66 *Glycine*
- 73 *Hypocalyptus*
- 75 *Kennedia*

V-SHAPED
- 18 *Bauhinia*

WEDGE
- 28 *Centrosema*
- 78 *Lathyrus*
- 82 *Lonchocarpus*
- 87 *Macroptilium*
- 132 *Swartzia*
- 139 *Vicia*
- 140 *Vigna*

HILUM POSITION

APICAL
- 2 *Acacia*
- 3 *Adenanthera*
- 6 *Afzelia*
- 7 *Albizia*
- 18 *Bauhinia*
- 20 *Brongniartia*
- 21 *Caesalpinia*
- 23 *Calliandra*
- 27 *Cassia*
- 50 *Dichrostachys*
- 54 *Entada*
- 55 *Enterolobium*
- 58 *Euchresta*
- 64 *Gleditsia*
- 68 *Gymnocladus*
- 104 *Parkia*
- 113 *Pithecellobium*
- 116 *Prosopis*
- 122 *Schrankia*
- 133 *Tamarindus*

SUBAPICAL
- 2 *Acacia*
- 7 *Albizia*
- 29 *Ceratonia*
- 30 *Cercis*
- 31 *Chamaecrista*
- 47 *Delonix*
- 48 *Desmanthus*
- 64 *Gleditsia*
- 71 *Hoffmannseggia*
- 72 *Hymenaea*
- 81 *Leucaena*
- 85 *Lysiloma*
- 91 *Mimosa*
- 92 *Mimozyganthus*
- 94 *Neptunia*
- 105 *Parkinsonia*
- 107 *Peltophorum*
- 124 *Senna*

HILUM POSITION

IN NOTCH
- 16 *Astragalus*
- 17 *Baptisia*
- 37 *Colutea*
- 41 *Crotalaria*
- 88 *Marina*
- 89 *Medicago*
- 90 *Melilotus*
- 95 *Nissolia*
- 98 *Ononis*
- 102 *Oxytropis*
- 106 *Parryella*

IN NOTCH (Cont.)
- 118 *Psorothamnus*
- 121 *Robinia*
- 128 *Sphaerophysa*
- 136 *Trifolium*
- 137 *Trigonella*
- 138 *Ulex*

ON SHOULDER
- 84 *Lupinus*

HILUM SURROUNDED BY:

COLLAR
- 4 *Adesmia*
- 13 *Anthyllis*
- 41 *Crotalaria*
- 49 *Desmodium*
- 52 *Diphysa*
- 59 *Eysenhardtia*
- 65 *Glottidium*
- 80 *Lespedeza*
- 84 *Lupinus*
- 86 *Maackia*
- 88 *Marina*
- 93 *Mucuna*
- 106 *Parryella*
- 111 *Piscidia*
- 114 *Podalyria*
- 117 *Psoralea*
- 118 *Psorothamnus*
- 120 *Rhyncosia*

EYE
- 5 *Aeschynomene*
- 13 *Anthyllis*
- 21 *Caesalpinia*
- 24 *Canavalia*
- 28 *Centrosema*
- 34 *Cladastris*
- 38 *Coronilla*
- 49 *Desmodium*

EYE (Cont.)
- 60 *Galactia*
- 66 *Glycine*
- 93 *Mucuna*
- 101 *Ornithopus*
- 109 *Phaseolus*
- 111 *Piscidia*
- 123 *Scorpiurus*
- 125 *Sesbania*
- 126 *Sophora*
- 127 *Spartium*
- 131 *Stylosanthes*
- 134 *Tephrosia*
- 140 *Vigna*
- 142 *Zornia*

RAPHE
- 27 *Cassia*
- 34 *Cladastris*
- 44 *Dalbergia*
- 49 *Desmodium*
- 56 *Errazurizia*
- 86 *Maackia*
- 98 *Ononis*
- 105 *Parkinsonia*
- 106 *Parryella*
- 114 *Podalyria*

ARIL

FLESHY
2 *Acacia*
6 *Afzelia*
19 *Bossiaea*
20 *Brongniartia*
46 *Daviesia*
75 *Kennedia*
76 *Lablab*
114 *Podalyria*
138 *Ulex*

RIM
22 *Cajanus*
35 *Clitoria*
36 *Cologania*
43 *Cytisus*
51 *Dioclea*
57 *Erythrina*
62 *Genista*
63 *Genistidium*
73 *Hypocalyptus*
77 *Laburnum*
97 *Onobrychis*
101 *Ornithopus*
102 *Oxytropis*

RIM (Cont.)
117 *Psoralea*
118 *Psorothamnus*
119 *Pueraria*
125 *Sesbania*
135 *Thermopsis*

TONGUE
14 *Apios*
24 *Canavalia*
28 *Centrosema*
40 *Cracca*
60 *Galactia*
66 *Glycine*
93 *Mucuna*
99 *Ophrestia*
103 *Pachyrrhizus*
108 *Peteria*
121 *Robinia*
127 *Spartium*
130 *Strophostyles*
134 *Tephrosia*
135 *Thermopsis*
141 *Wisteria*

Abrus Adanson
Abreae, Faboideae

Species: *precatorius* Linnaeus.

Common Names: Jequirity-bean, precatory-bean, rosary-pea, crab's-eye.

Seed 6-8 x 4-5 x 4-5 mm, ovate, terete, glossy, bicolored with two-thirds scarlet becoming dull red with age and one-third black, smooth, with elliptic marginal hilum concealed by whitish funicular remnant.

Notes: Woody vine of tropical Asia, naturalized in waste ground of Florida. Seeds are deadly poisonous when eaten by humans, and interstate shipment and importation into the United States of seeds are forbidden by law. Because of their striking color, seeds often are made into necklaces and other seed jewelry, a practice which is strongly discouraged.

Acacia Miller
Acacieae, Mimosoideae

Species: *angustissima* (P. Miller) O. Kuntze var. *hirta* (Nuttall) B. L. Robinson.

Common Names: Prairie acacia, fern acacia.

Seed 4-5.5 x 3-5 x 1-2 mm, elliptic to circular, flattened, dull, reddish brown mottled with darker reddish brown, bearing 90% pleurogram on each face and punctiform apical hilum.

Notes: Herbaceous perennial of Florida (apparently disjunctly) and Missouri and Nebraska, south to Louisiana and Texas. Variety *hirta* is one of seven U.S. varieties, all browsed by livestock. The species ranges from herbs to shrubs and occurs from Florida to Missouri and Arizona.

Acacia Miller
Acacieae, Mimosoideae

Species: *cyclops* A. Cunningham ex G. Don.

Common Name: Acacia.

Seed 5-6 x 3-4 x 2-2.5 mm (excluding aril), oblong, compressed, glossy, dark reddish brown, with 90% pleurogram on each face and punctiform subapical hilum usually concealed by bright yellowish-orange aril that may partially or completely surround the seed.

Notes: Shrub to small tree of Australia, cultivated in urban California.

Acacia Miller
Acacieae, Mimosoideae

Species: *decurrens* (Wendland) Willdenow.

Common Name: Green wattle acacia.

Seed: 3.5-5 x 2.5-3 x 1.7-2 mm, oblong, compressed, glossy, dark reddish brown, with 90% pleurogram and fracture lines on each face and punctiform subapical hilum concealed by tan oblique aril.

Notes: Tree of Australia, cultivated as a fast-growing tree in California.

Abrus precatorius 4.8X

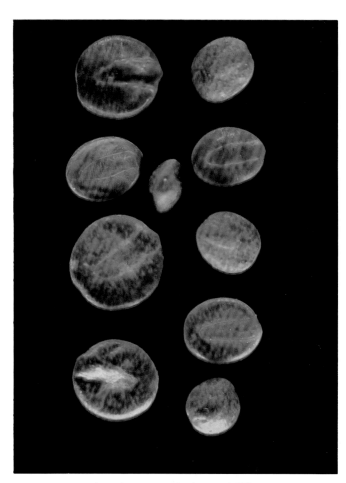

Acacia angustissima 4.8X

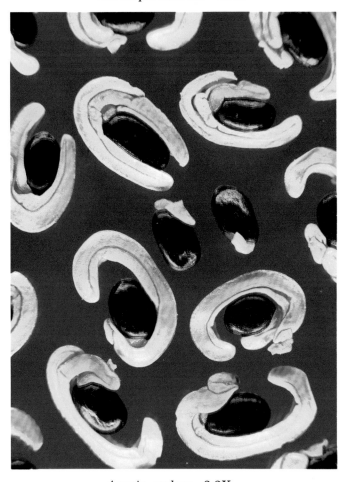

Acacia cyclops 3.2X

Acacia decurrens 7.2X

15

Acacia Miller
Acacieae, Mimosoideae

Species: *farnesiana* (Linnaeus) Willdenow.

Common Names: Sweet acacia, cassie, huisache.

Seed 7-8.5 x 6-7.5 x 3-5 mm, circular to oblong, compressed, dull, dark reddish brown, with 90% pleurogram on each face and punctiform apical hilum.

Notes: Spiny shrub to small tree of tropical America, cultivated in Florida and California. Cassie perfume is distilled from the flowers, especially around Cannes, France.

Acacia Miller
Acacieae, Mimosoideae

Species: *toruosa* (Linnaeus) Willdenow.

Common Name: Twisted acacia.

Seed 7-10 x 4-5 x 3-4 mm, oblong, compressed, glossy, dark brown with lighter colored areole, with 100% pleurogram on each face and punctiform subapical hilum concealed by caplike aril.

Notes: Shrub to small tree of the coastal strand of south Florida. *Acacia toruosa* auct. of Texas has been excluded from this species (Isely, 1973).

Adenanthera Linnaeus
Mimoseae, Mimosoideae

Species: *pavonina* Linnaeus.

Common Name: Red sandlewood.

Seed 9-10 x 9-10 x 6-6.5 mm, nearly circular, nearly compressed, glossy, scarlet to red, with 90% pleurogram and reticulate fracture lines on each face and punctiform apical hilum.

Notes: Tree of Asia, cultivated in south Florida. Seeds are used in seed jewelry.

Adesmia de Candolle
Adesmieae, Faboideae

Species: *incana* Vogel.

Common Name: Adesmia.

Seed 2-2.5 x 2-2.5 x 1.9-2.1 mm, D-shaped, slightly compressed, glossy, reddish brown and faintly dark reddish brown to tan and conspicuously streaked and mottled with dark brown, smooth, with circular marginal hilum surrounded by whitish collar.

Notes: Herbaceous perennial not present in the United States. This species was selected to represent the monotypic tribe Adesmieae with 230 species native of southern South America.

Acacia farenesiana 3.2X

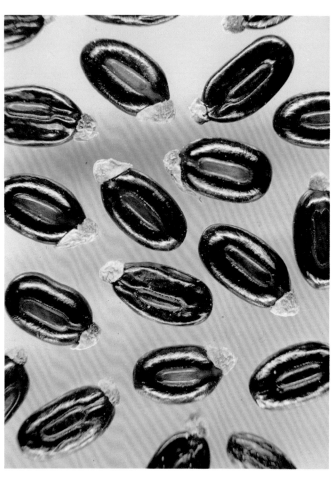

Acacia toruosa 3.2X

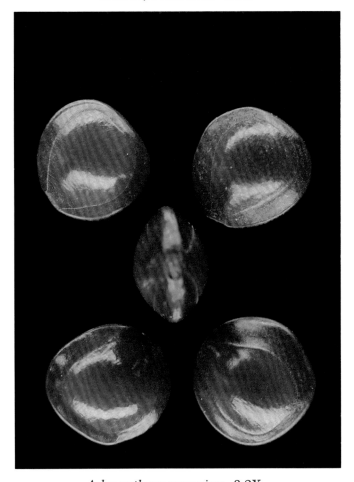

Adenanthera pavonina 3.2X

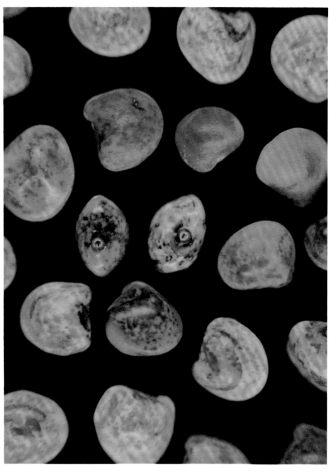

Adesmia incana 9.6X

Aeschynomene Linnaeus
Aeschynomeneae, Faboideae

Species: *indica* Linnaeus.

Common Names: Indian jointvetch, ding.

Seed 3.2-4 x 2-2.5 x 1.5-1.8 mm, D- to C-shaped, somewhat compressed, glossy, reddish brown, smooth, with oblong marginal hilum surrounded by faint eye. Loment 5-6.5 x 4-4.5 x 2.3-2.5 mm, nearly square (if basal or apical segment, one end will be rounded), dull reddish brown, area over seed chamber often tuberculate.

Notes: Herbaceous annual of moist ground from North Carolina south to Florida and west to Texas.

Afzelia Smith
Detarieae, Caesalpinioideae

Species: *quanzensis* Welwitsch.

Common Name: Afzelia.

Seed 25-30 x 11-16 x 9-12 mm, oblong, more or less terete, semiglossy, black, smooth, with punctiform apical hilum often concealed by thick yellow to orange caplike aril.

Notes: Tree not present in the United States. This species was selected to represent the large and primarily African woody tribe Detarieae. Seeds of various species, including this one, are used in seed jewelry.

Albizia Durazzini
Ingeae, Mimosoideae

Species: *julibrissin* Durazzini.

Common Name: Mimosa, silktree.

Seed 6.5-7.5 x 4-5 x 2 mm, oblong, compressed, semiglossy, reddish brown, with 90% pleurogram and concentric fracture lines on each face, with punctiform subapical hilum.

Notes: Tree of Asia, cultivated and naturalized along roadsides and in open woodlands from New York to Missouri, south to Florida, Texas and California.

Albizia Durazzini
Ingeae, Mimosoideae

Species: *lebbeck* (Linnaeus) Bentham.

Common Name: Woman's tongue tree.

Seed 7-10 x 6-7 x 2 mm, nearly circular, compressed, semiglossy, reddish brown, with 100% pleurogram and reticulate fracture lines (in areole and just beyond pleurogram) on each face and punctiform apical hilum.

Notes: Tree of Asia, cultivated and escaped from south Florida to Texas and California.

Aeschynomene indica 4.8X

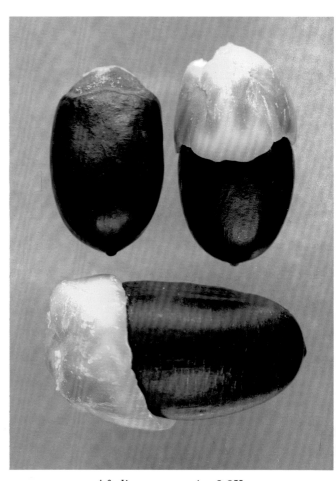

Afzelia quanzensis 3.2X

Albizia julibrissin 4.8X

Albizia lebbeck 3.2X

Alhagi Adanson
Galegeae, Faboideae

Species: *maurorum* Medikus subsp. *maurorum.*

Common Name: Camelthorn.

Seed 2.5-3 x 1.9-2.3 x 1 mm, oblong, compressed, dull, reddish to greenish brown and some mottled with darker brown, smooth, with punctiform marginal hilum concealed by whitish funicular remnant. Loment 5-6 x 3-3 x 3-3 mm, oblong, terete, dull, reddish tan, rugose.

Notes: Shrub of Asia, naturalized along drainage ditches and streams from Texas to California. In U.S. floras, this noxious weed is known either as *A. pseudalhagi* (M. Bieberstein) Desvaux or *A. camelorum* Fischer.

Alysicarpus Desvaux
Desmodieae, Faboideae

Species: *vaginalis* (Linnaeus) de Candolle.

Common Names: Alyce-clover, buffalo-clover.

Seed 1.5-2 x 1-1.5 x 1-1.2 mm, ovate, compressed, glossy, yellow to reddish brown and sometimes mottled with darker reddish brown, smooth, with punctiform marginal hilum.

Notes: Herbaceous perennial of tropical Asia, naturalized in waste ground and cultivated for hay, cover crop or pasture along Gulf Coast from Florida to Texas.

Amorpha Linnaeus
Amorpheae, Faboideae

Species: *canescens* Pursh.

Common Names: Leadplant, leadplant amorpha, shoestrings.

Seed 2-2.7 x 1-1.5 x 0.8-1 mm, oblong, compressed, glossy, reddish to yellowish brown, smooth, with circular marginal hilum. One-seeded indehiscent fruit 3.6-4 x 2-2.4 x 2 mm, falcate, terete, dull, reddish brown, densely covered with gray hairs and glandularly dotted, with persistent calyx.

Notes: Herbaceous perennial in rocky open woods or sandy prairies from Michigan to Saskatchewan, south to Indiana, Illinois, Arkansas, Texas, and New Mexico. Leadplant is a palatable range plant that also is cultivated as an ornamental.

Amorpha Linnaeus
Amorpheae, Faboideae

Species: *fruticosa* Linnaeus.

Common Names: False-indigo, bastard-indigo, indigobush.

Seed 3.5-4 x 1.1-1.5 x 1 mm, falcate, compressed, glossy, greenish to reddish tan to reddish brown, smooth, with oblong marginal hilum. One-seeded indehiscent fruit 6-8 x 2-2.5 x 1.5-2 mm, falcate, nearly terete, dull, tan to brown with dark brown to reddish brown glands, with persistent calyx.

Notes: Shrub in moist woods and along stream banks from Pennsylvania to Minnesota and Saskatchewan, south from Alabama to Wyoming and California. Four varieties are recognized in the United States.

Alhagi maurorum 7.2X

Alysicarpus vaginalis 9.6X

Amorpha canescens 9.6X

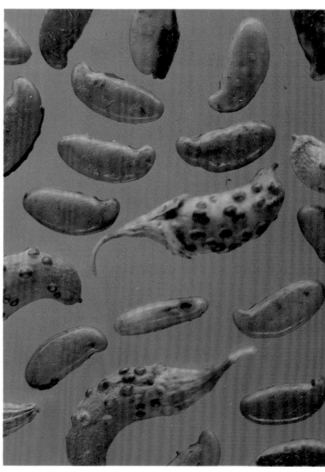

Amorpha fruticosa 6.4X

Amphicarpaea Elliott

Glycininae, Phaseoleae, Faboideae

Species: *bracteata* (Linnaeus) Fernald.

Common Name: Hog-peanut.

Seed 2.4-3.2 x 2.3-2.7 x 1.8-2 mm, elliptic, compressed, dull, dark brown to black with some mottles, smooth, with oblong marginal hilum concealed by white funicular remnant.

Notes: Herbaceous perennial vine of woods and thickets, Nova Scotia to Manitoba and Montana, south to Florida and Texas. Plants produce three fruit types: Aerial dehiscent three-four-seeded dry fruits, above ground dehiscent one-seeded fleshy fruits, and subterranean indehiscent one-seeded fruits. The latter fruits are edible and resemble garden bean in taste. Two varieties are recognized in the United States: Var. *bracteata* and var. *comosa* (Linnaeus) Fernald. The latter variety may be regarded as a separate species, *A. pitcheri* A Gray. The genus name is often incorrectly spelled *Amphicarpea*.

Andira Jussieu

Dalbergieae, Faboideae

Species: *inermis* (W. Wright) Kunth.

Common Names: Angelin, angelintree.

One-seeded endocarp 40 x 30 x 30 mm, oblong, terete, dull, grayish brown, rugose, with encircling longitudinal ridge.

Notes: Native tree of tropical America, naturalized and cultivated on the Florida Keys. Free seeds are seldom found in nature.

Anthyllis Linnaeus

Loteae, Faboideae

Species: *vulneraria* Linnaeus.

Common Names: Kidneyvetch, false moneywort.

Seed 2-5 x 1.5-1.7 x 1 mm, oblong, subterete, to compressed, glossy, bicolored, three-quarters reddish brown to yellow and one-quarter greenish, smooth, with punctiform marginal hilum concealed or not by whitish funicular remnant and surrounded by whitish collar and dark eye. Loment 3.5-4 x 2.5-3 x 1.5 mm, D-shaped, compressed, dull, straw colored, reticulate.

Notes: Herbaceous perennial to annual of Eurasia, adventive in northern United States and California. Kidneyvetch, a species complex containing numerous subspecies, has been introduced as a crop several times.

Apios Fabricus

Erythrininae, Phaseoleae, Faboideae

Species: *americana* Medikus.

Common Names: American groundnut, American potatobean, Indian-potato.

Seed 5-5.5 x 4-5 x 3-4 mm, oblong, subterete, glossy, dark reddish brown, rugose, with oblong marginal hilum bearing tongue-aril.

Notes: Herbaceous perennial vine in moist woods and meadows from Quebec to North Dakota, south to Florida and Texas. Rhizomes bear a row of two or more edible tubers.

Amphicarpaea bracteata 7.2X

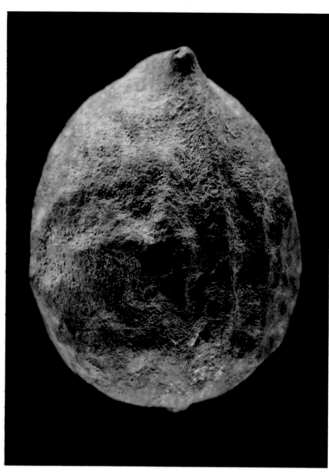

Andira inermis 3.2X

Anthyllis vulneraria 9.6X

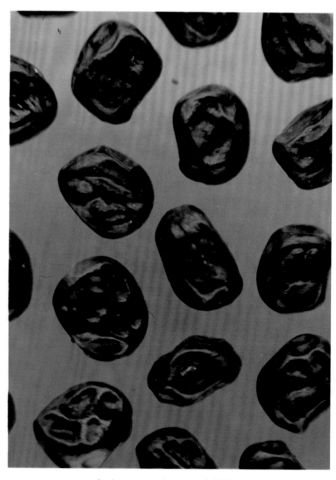

Apios americana 4.8X

Arachis Linnaeus
Aeschynomeneae, Faboideae

Species: *hypogaea* Linnaeus.

Common Names: Peanut, earthnut, goober, groundnut, pindar.

Seed 10-35 x 5-15 x 5-15 mm, oblong to ovate, terete, dull, color usually reddish brown, (other colors listed below), rugose, with punctiform marginal hilum concealed by white funicular remnant. One- to five-seeded indehiscent fruits up to 100 mm and 10-20 mm in diameter, oblong, terete, dull, ochre to brown, reticulate.

Notes: Herbaceous annual of South America, widely planted and escaped from Delaware to Kansas, south to Florida and Texas. One of the ten most important legumes in United States agriculture, producing edible seeds and oil as well as foliage used for forage and silage. Seed coat colors other than reddish brown are monochrome pink, red, purple, tan, brown, yellow, and white or bichrome purple and white or mottled purple over one of the above mentioned colors. Seed coat color may be useful in cultivar identification (Duke, 1981).

Astragalus Linnaeus
Galegeae, Faboideae

Species: *canadensis* Linnaeus.

Common Names: Canada milk-vetch, Canadian rattleweed.

Seed 1.7-2 x 1.5-1.8 x 1 mm, mitten shaped, compressed, semiglossy, tan, smooth, with punctiform marginal hilum partially concealed by whitish funicular ring.

Notes: Herbaceous perennial occurring in a variety of habitats from the lower St. Lawrence River west to northern Rocky Mountains and Great and Columbia Basins, south to the Appalachians and Gulf Coast of east Texas and California. Three varieties are recognized in the United States.

Astragalus Linnaeus
Galegeae, Faboideae

Species: *crassicarpus* Nuttall var. *crassicarpus*.

Common Names: Ground-plum, buffalo-plum, pomme de prairie.

Seed 5-6.5 x 5.5-6.5 x 1 mm, mitten shaped, compressed, dull, black, smooth, with punctiform hilum in notch and concealed by white funicular remnant.

Notes: Herbaceous perennial of prairies, roadsides, railroad rights of way and old pastures from the Mississippi River west to Montana and Arizona. Succulent raw indehiscent fruits resembling green plums are not appetizing though boiling may improve taste (Barneby, 1964). Five varieties are recognized in the United States. Previously known as *Astragalus caryocarpus* Ker.

Astragalus Linnaeus
Galegeae, Faboideae

Species: *drummondii* Douglas ex Hooker.

Common Name: Drummond milk-vetch.

Seed 2.5-3.5 x 1.5-2 x 0.5 mm, mitten shaped, compressed, glossy, blackish brown to brown or tan, conspicuously pitted, with punctiform hilum in notch and concealed by funicular remnant.

Notes: Herbaceous perennial of grasslands and brushlands from Saskatchewan to Alberta, south to New Mexico and Nevada.

Arachis hypogaea 2.8X

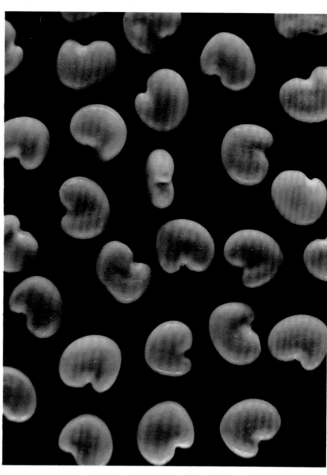

Astragalus canadensis 9.6X

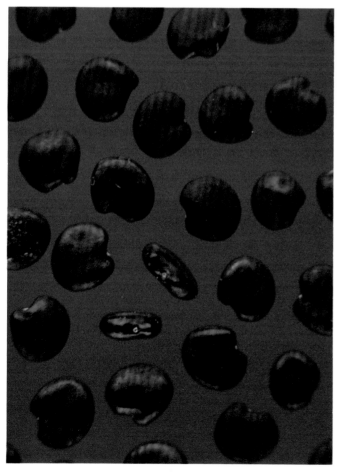

Astragalus crassicarpus 7.2X

Astragalus drummondii 9.6X

25

Astragalus Linnaeus
Galegeae, Faboideae

Species: *purshii* Douglas ex Hooker.
Common Names: Pursh milk-vetch, tufted loco.
Seed 2.2-2.8 x 2-2.3 x 1 mm, mitten shaped, compressed, dull, black or reddish brown to tan, smooth to variably pitted or rarely rugose, with punctiform hilum in notch and concealed by whitish funicular remnant.
Notes: Herbaceous perennial on dry hills and plains from North Dakota to Alberta, south to the head of the North Platte, Grand, and Yampa Rivers, Utah and California. Nine varieties are recognized in the United States.

Baptisia Ventenat
Thermopsideae, Faboideae

Species: *australis* (Linnaeus) R. Brown.
Common Names: Blue false-indigo, blue wild-indigo.
Seed 4-5 x 2.5-3.2 x 2 mm, falcate, compressed, glossy to dull, dark brown to tan, covered with grayish film and bearing tuberculate-like exudate, with circular hilum in notch.
Notes: Herbaceous perennial in grassy areas from Vermont, south to Georgia and the Ohio River valley and Iowa, west to Texas. Two varieties are recognized in United States: Var. *australis* from Iowa to Texas and var. *minor* Lehmann east of the Mississippi River.

Bauhinia Linnaeus
Cercideae, Caesalpinioideae

Species: *monarda* Kurz.
Common Name: Pink orchidtree.
Seed 10-13 x 9-12 x 3-4 mm, nearly circular, compressed, semiglossy, reddish brown and usually with darker center on each face, rugose, with linear apical hilum concealed by funicular remnant.
Notes: Tree of southeastern Asia, cultivated in subtropical Florida.

Bauhinia Linnaeus
Cercideae, Caesalpinioideae

Species: *tomentosa* Linnaeus.
Common Name: Bauhinia.
Seed 7-8.5 x 5.5-7 x 2-3 mm, ovate or nearly so, compressed, glossy, reddish brown, somewhat rugose to nearly smooth, with V-shaped marginal hilum often bearing an apical hook-shaped funicular remnant.
Notes: Tree of Old World, cultivated in South Florida and urban California.

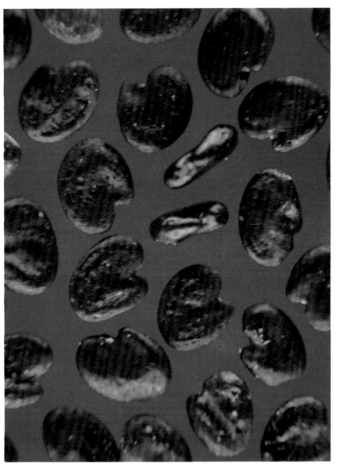

Astragalus purshii 9.6X

Baptisia australis 7.2X

Bauhinia monarda 3.2X

Bauhinia tomentosa 3.2X

Bossiaea Ventenat
Bossiaeeae, Faboideae

Species: *heterophylla* Ventenat.

Common Name: Variable bossea.

Seed: 3-3.5 x 2.2-2.5 x 2 mm, oblong, compressed, dull, dark reddish brown to blackish, smooth, with oblong marginal hilum concealed by honey-colored hooked aril.

Notes: A shrub to undershrub which is not present in the United States. Variable bossea was selected to represent the 10-genus tribe Bossiaeeae with a natural distribution limited to Australia.

Brongniartia Kunth
Brongniartieae, Faboideae

Species: *minutiflora* S. Watson.

Common Name: Texas brongniarta.

Seed 8 x 7 x 2.5 mm, circular, compressed, glossy, tan, smooth with circular apical hilum concealed by whitish tan aril.

Notes: Shrub of southern Brewster County, Texas and Chihuahua, Mexico. Only one seed was obtained and studied.

Caesalpinia Linnaeus
Caesalpinieae, Caesalpinioideae

Species: *bonduc* (Linnaeus) Roxburgh.

Common Names: Graynicker, gray nickernut.

Seed 23-25 x 20-22 x 15-18 mm, circular or nearly so, terete, dull, gray, with concentric fracture lines and punctiform apical hilum surrounded by conspicuous dark eye.

Notes: Reclining prickly shrub of coastal peninsular Florida. Seeds drift in warm sea currents (Gunn, Dennis, and Paradine, 1976).

Caesalpinia Linnaeus
Caesalpinieae, Caesalpinioideae

Species: *coriacea* (Jacquin) Willdenow.

Common Name: Divi-divi.

Seed 5-6 x 3-4 x 1.5 mm, ovate to oblong, compressed, glossy, reddish brown, with concentric fracture lines and punctiform apical hilum surrounded by darker eye.

Notes: Shrub to small tree of tropical America, cultivated in southern Florida. Divi-divi pods are an important source of tannin in tropical America and India (Duke, 1981).

Bossiaea heterophylla 7.2X

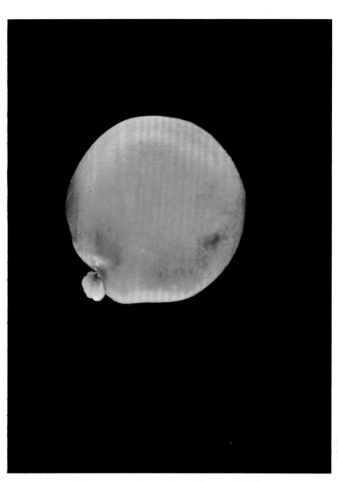

Brongniartia minutiflora 7.2X

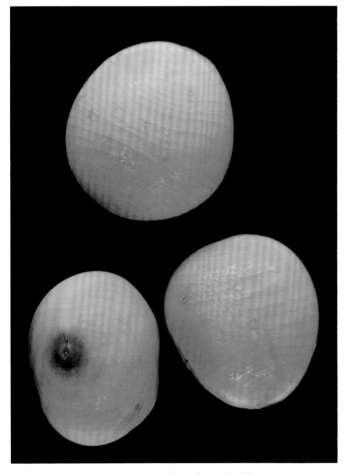

Caesalpinia bonduc 3.2X

Caesalpinia coriacea 4.8X

29

Caesalpinia Linnaeus
Caesalpinieae, Caesalpiniodeae
Species: *gilliesii* (Wallich ex W. J. Hooker) A. Dietrich.
Common Name: Bird-of-paradise.
Seed 11-14 x 10-13 x 2-3 mm, subcordate, nearly flattened, glossy, reddish brown mottled and streaked with dark reddish brown, rugose, with concentric fracture lines and punctiform apical hilum concealed by whitish funicular remnant.
Notes: Tree to shrub of Argentina, cultivated and naturalized in disturbed and rural areas from Texas to California.

Caesalpinia Linnaeus
Caesalpinieae, Caesalpiniodeae
Species: *pulcherrima* (Linnaeus) Swartz.
Common Name: Poinciana.
Seed 13 x 10-12 x 7 mm, triangular to irregularly shaped, compressed, semiglossy, dark reddish brown, with concentric fracture lines and punctiform apical hilum concealed by brownish funicular remnant.
Notes: Unarmed to slightly prickled shrub to small tree of tropical America, cultivated and occasionally naturalized from Florida to Arizona, and probably California.

Caesalpinia Linnaeus
Caesalpinieae, Caesalpiniodeae
Species: *sappan* Linnaeus.
Common Names: Sappanwood, Indian-redwood, false-sandlewood, Indian brazilwood.
Seed 15-18 x 9-10 x 5-8 mm, oblong or nearly so, compressed, semiglossy, brown, with concentric fracture lines and punctiform apical hilum concealed by whitish funicular remnant.
Notes: Tree of Asia, cultivated in subtropical Florida. Wood is source of valuable red dye for fabrics and is the redwood or brazilwood of commerce.

Cajanus de Candolle
Cajaninae, Phaseoleae, Faboideae
Species: *cajan* (Linnaeus) Huth.
Common Names: Pigeon-pea, no-eye-pea, red-gram.
Seed 7-10 x 7-9 x 6-7 mm, oblong, compressed, dull, whitish gray mottled with dark reddish brown, faintly pitted, with oblong marginal hilum with rim-aril and surrounded by reddish brown halo.
Notes: Woody shrub, mostly treated as an annual in cultivation, of the Old World tropics, naturalized in south Florida. Green seeds and pods may be consumed as a nutritious vegetable. Pigeon-pea is listed in some floras as *Cajanus indicus* Sprengel.

Caesalpinia gilliesii 3.2X

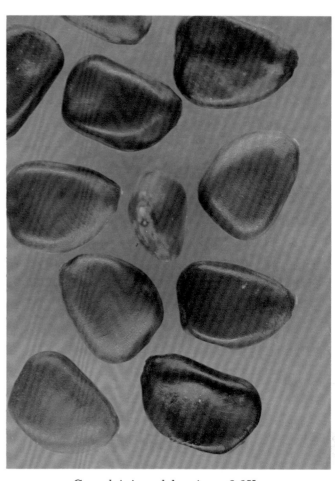

Caesalpinia pulcherrima 3.2X

Caesalpinia sappan 3.2X

Cajanus cajan 3.2X

31

Calliandra Bentham
Ingeae, Mimosoideae

Species: *eriophylla* Bentham.

Common Names: Fairy duster, mesquitella, mock-mesquite, false-mesquite.

Seed 5.5-7.5 x 3-4 x 2-3 mm, narrowly ovate, compressed, semiglossy, grayish brown mottled lightly or densely with black, with 1 prominent longitudinal ridge on each face and punctiform apical hilum concealed by funicular remnant.

Notes: Shrub of rocky desert slopes from western New Mexico to southern California. Two varieties are recognized in the United States: Var. *chamaedrys* Isely, a rare plant of Uvalde Co., Texas and var. *eriophylla*.

Calliandra Bentham
Ingeae, Mimosoideae

Species: *humilis* Bentham.

Common Name: Small false-mesquite.

Seed 5-6 x 3-4 x 1.5-2 mm, oblong with attenuate apex, compressed, semiglossy, grayish tan mottled with darker brown, with 90% pleurogram on each face and punctiform apical hilum exposed to concealed by funicular remnant.

Notes: Herbaceous perennial of rocky soils, grasslands, or pine forests of west Texas to Arizona. Two varieties are recognized in the United States: Var. *humilis* and var. *reticulata* (A. Gray) L. Benson.

Canavalia de Candolle
Diocleinae, Phaseoleae, Faboideae

Species: *ensiformis* (Linnaeus) de Candolle.

Common Names: Jack-bean, chicksaw-lima, overlook-bean, Pearson-bean, wonder-bean.

Seed 14-22 x 12-16 x 7-10 mm, oblong, compressed, semiglossy, ivory to white, smooth, with oblong marginal hilum with tongue-aril and surrounded by brown eye.

Notes: Herbaceous annual vine to bushlike of tropical America, in limited cultivation in southern United States. Mature dry seeds are poisonous to humans and should not be eaten unless cooked for a long time and seed coat removed. The seed coat contains a mild poison (Duke, 1981). Seeds and young indehiscent fruits, when less than 15 cm long, may be cooked and eaten.

Caragana Fabricius
Galegeae, Faboideae

Species: *arborescens* Lamarck.

Common Names: Siberian peashrub, caragana peatree.

Seed 3.5-4.5 x 2.5-3.2 x 2.5-3.2 mm, oblong to irregularly oblong and indented (because of pressure of adjacent seeds in pods), terete or nearly so, semiglossy, dark reddish brown, usually faintly pitted and occasionally faintly striate, with punctiform marginal hilum concealed by whitish funicular remnant.

Notes: Small tree of Siberia and Manchuria, cultivated and naturalized in sandy, alkaline soils from North Dakota to Iowa.

Calliandra eriophylla 4.8X

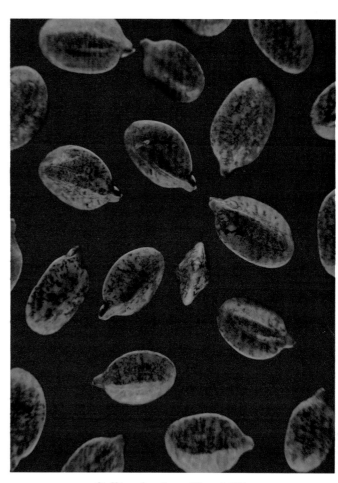

Calliandra humilis 4.8X

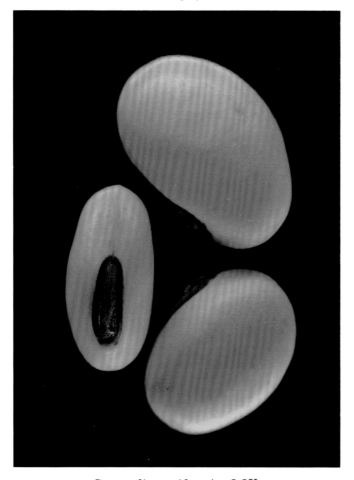

Canavalia ensiformis 3.2X

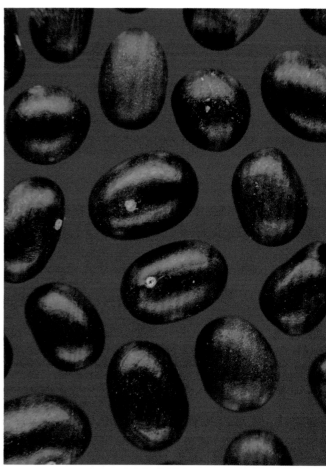

Caragana arborescens 7.2X

33

Carmichaelia R. Brown
Carmichaelieae, Faboideae

Species: *arenaria* G. Simpson.

Common Name: Carmichaelia.

Seed 2-2.5 x 1.5 x 1 mm, oblong to mitten shaped or with one straight side, compressed, glossy, light to dark reddish brown mottled with black streaks (as seeds darken with age mottles less conspicuous), smooth, with circular marginal hilum occasionally concealed by funicular remnant.

Notes: Carmichaelia, a shrub not present in the United States, was selected to represent the tribe Carmichaelieae composed of small trees, shrubs, or subshrubs in five genera in New Zealand, Philip Island, and Lord Howe Island.

Cassia Linnaeus
Cassieae, Caesalpinioideae

Species: *fistula* Linnaeus.

Common Name: Golden shower.

Seed 15-17 x 8-10 x 3-3.5 mm, oblong, compressed, dull, reddish tan to reddish brown, smooth, with one dark line or ridge on one face, with punctiform apical hilum on one face and subtended or not by dark linear raphe.

Notes: Tree of southeastern Asia, cultivated in southern Florida and California. Seeds of *Cassia* spp., including *C. fistula* and *C. javanica,* are unusual in the family because they are compressed at right angles to the cotyledonary plane. The hilum and raphe appear on the face (one face only) and not on the margin as they do in most other legume seeds.

Cassia Linnaeus
Cassieae, Caesalpinioideae

Species: *javanica* Linnaeus.

Common Name: Pink shower.

Seed 7-7.5 x 6-7 x 3-4 mm, circular or nearly so, compressed, glossy, reddish brown, with reticulate fracture lines and punctiform apical hilum on one face and subtended by dark linear raphe.

Notes: Tree of southeastern Asia, cultivated in southern Florida. For a seed note, see *Cassia fistula.*

Centrosema (de Candolle) Bentham
Clitoriinae, Phaseoleae, Faboideae

Species: *virginiana* (Linnaeus) Bentham.

Common Name: Spurred butterfly-pea.

Seed 3.5-4.2 x 2-2.5 x 2 mm, rectangular, nearly terete, dull, reddish to tannish brown mottled with blackish and ochre, smooth, with wedge-shaped marginal hilum and with or without tongue-aril surrounded by blackish eye.

Notes: Herbaceous perennial of dry sandy woods from New Jersey to Kentucky, south to Florida and Texas.

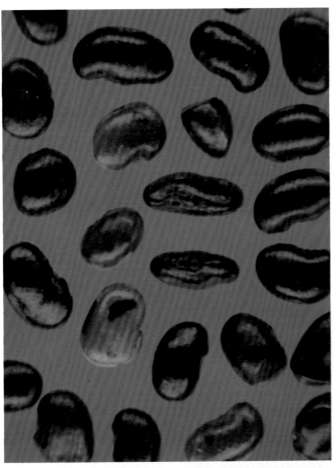

Carmichaelia arenaria 9.6X

Cassia fistula 3.2X

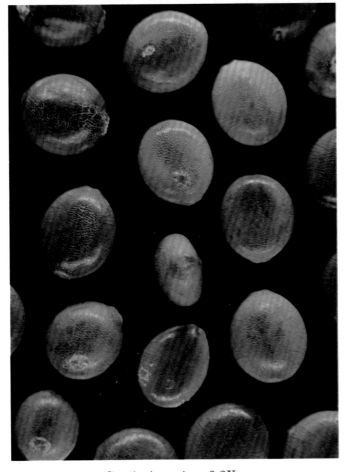

Cassia javanica 3.2X

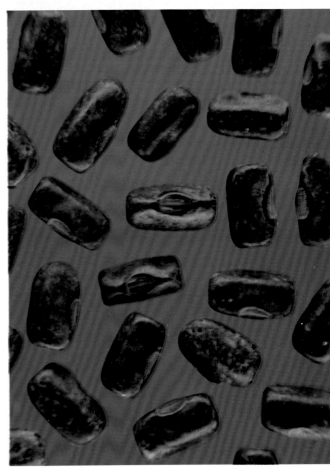

Centrosema virginiana 6.4X

Ceratonia Linnaeus
Cassieae, Caesalpinioideae

Species: *siliqua* Linnaeus.

Common Names: Carob, carob-bean, locust-bean, John's bread, St. John's bread.

Seed 8-9 x 6-7 x 4 mm, irregularly ovate, compressed, semiglossy, reddish brown, with inconspicuous reticulate fracture lines and minutely punctate or not, with punctiform subapical hilum in notch and usually concealed by honey-colored funicular remnant.

Notes: Dioecious tree of eastern Mediterranean region, is cultivated in Florida, Texas, Arizona, and urban California. This is the biblical carob whose pods and seeds are used for human food (high sugar and calcium content), as a substitute for chocolate, as a stabilizer, and in livestock feeds, especially for cattle.

Cercis Linnaeus
Cercideae, Caesalpinioideae

Species: *canadensis* Linnaeus.

Common Name: Redbud.

Seed 5-6.5 x 3.5-4.3 x 2 mm, oblong, compressed, glossy to dull, reddish brown, faint striations radiating from center of each face, with punctiform subapical hilum.

Notes: Small tree to shrub of rich woods and ravines from Massachusetts south to Florida and to Iowa, Nebraska, Oklahoma, and Texas and cultivated within and beyond natural range. Three varieties are recognized in the United States.

Chamaecrista (Linnaeus) Moench
Cassieae, Caesalpinioideae

Species: *absus* (Linnaeus) Irwin & Barneby.

Common Name: Chamaecrista.

Seed 4-5 x 3.5-4.5 x 2 mm, rectangular to regularly or irregularly ovate, compressed, glossy, reddish brown to reddish black, with longitudinally aligned pits and punctiform subapical hilum.

Notes: Herbaceous annual on granite mountain slopes and barely reaching the United States in Pima and Santa Cruz Counties, Arizona. Recently published U.S. floras and Isely (1975) placed this species in *Cassia,* but Irwin and Barneby (1982) returned it to the genus *Chamaecrista.*

Chamaecrista (Linnaeus) Moench
Cassieae, Caesalpinioideae

Species: *fasciculata* (Michaux) Greene.

Common Name: Wild-sensitive plant.

Seed 3.3-4 x 2.7-4 x 1 mm, rectangular to square or irregular and with one attenuate corner, compressed, semiglossy, blackish brown, with longitudinally aligned pits and punctiform subapical hilum often concealed by funicular remnant.

Notes: Herbaceous annual in diverse dry disturbed habitats from Massachusetts to Nebraska, south to Florida and Texas. See Notes under *Chamaecrista absus* for a discussion of the genus name.

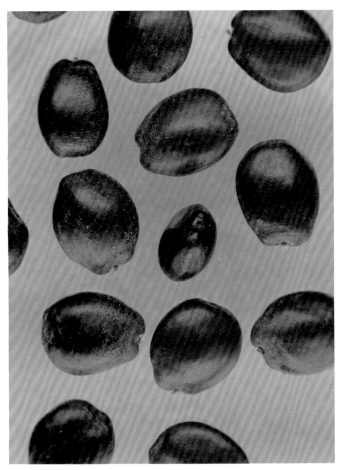

Ceratonia siliqua 3.2X

Cercis canadensis 4.8X

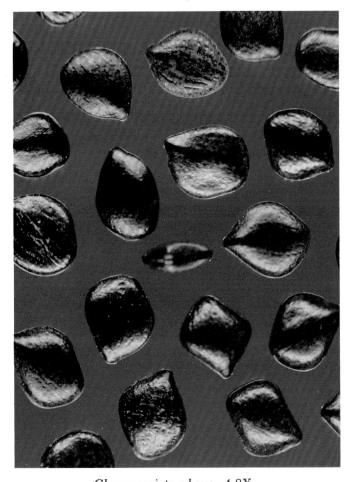

Chamaecrista absus 4.8X

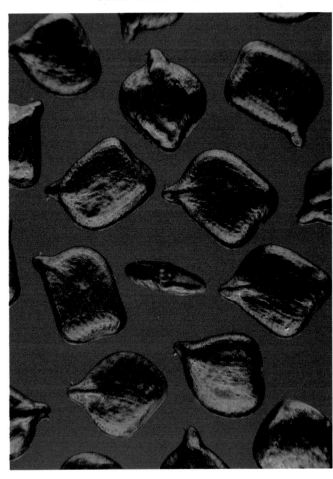

Chamaecrista fasciculata 7.2X

Chamaecrista (Linnaeus) Moench
Cassieae, Caesalpinioideae

Species: *nictitans* (Linnaeus) Moench.
Common Name: Wild-sensitive plant.
Seed 3-3.3 x 2-2.5 x 1 mm, square to irregular shaped with one attenuate corner, compressed, glossy, dark reddish brown, with reticulate fracture lines and with or without longitudinal aligned pits, with punctiform subapical hilum often concealed by reddish brown funicular remnant.
Notes: Herbaceous annual in diverse dry disturbed habitats from Massachusetts to Nebraska, south to Florida and Texas. See Notes under *Chamaecrista absus*.

Chapmannia Torrey & Gray
Aeschynomeneae, Faboideae

Species: *floridana* Torrey & Gray.
Common Name: Alicia.
Seed 3.5-5.5 x 2-2.5 x 2-3 mm, ovate to oblong, compressed, dull, tan to yellowish, faintly rugose, with punctiform marginal hilum. Loment 6-7 x 2.5-3 x 2-2.5 mm, elliptic with one or two truncate whitish ends, subterete, dull, reddish to greenish or yellowish brown, with eglandular and glandular hairs and 9-14 ribs.
Notes: Herbaceous perennial of sandy woods of central and south Florida.

Cicer Linnaeus
Cicereae, Faboideae

Species: *arietinum* Linnaeus.
Common Names: Chickpea, garbanzo, Idaho-pea, gypsy-pea.
Seed 5-15 x 4-9 x 6-7 mm, ovate to angular, terete, dull, white to buff or yellowish with orange tint to brown or black or green, rugose to tuberculate, with circular marginal hilum.
Notes: Herbaceous annual of southwest Asia, cultivated mainly in California for its edible seeds.

Cladratis Rafinesque
Sophoreae, Faboideae

Species: *lutea* (Michaux) Koch.
Common Names: Yellow-wood, American yellow-wood, virgilia.
Seed 6-7 x 3-3.5 x 1.5-2 mm, oblong, compressed, dull, reddish brown, smooth, with circular marginal hilum partially concealed by whitish funicular remnant and surrounded by darker eye and subtended by darker raphe and lens.
Notes: Tree of rich woods from southern Indiana south to Georgia, Mississippi, and Oklahoma and occasionally planted as an ornamental tree within and beyond its natural range. Yellow-wood produces close-grained hard wood which is a source of yellow dye and occasionally used in gunstocks.

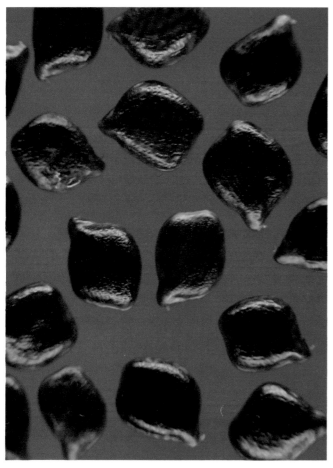

Chamaecrista nictitans 9.7X

Chapmannia floridana 7.2X

Cicer arietinum 3.2X

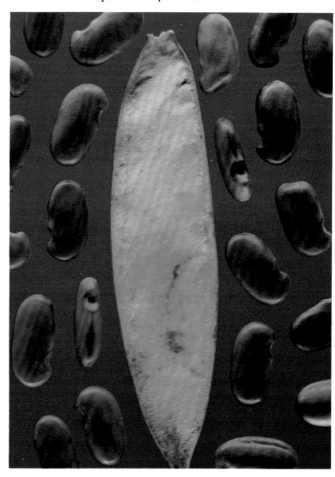

Cladratis lutea 4.0X

39

Clitoria Linnaeus
Clitoriinae, Phaseoleae, Faboideae

Species: *ternatea* Linnaeus.

Common Names: Blue-peas, blue-pea.

Seed 6-7 x 5 x 1.5-2 mm, oblong to subreniform, compressed, dull, reddish brown mottled with black (mottles may coalesce creating blackish seed coat), smooth, with oblong marginal hilum partially concealed by rim-aril (almost tonguelike).

Notes: Herbaceous perennial vine of Old World tropics, naturalized in pinelands and hammocks of southern Florida (Everglades and Florida Keys). Seeds yield a blue dye, and plants are used as a biennial ornamental cover crop (Duke, 1981).

Cologania Kunth
Glycininae, Phaseoleae, Faboideae

Species: *angustifolia* Kunth.

Common Name: Cologania.

Seed 2.5-3 x 2.5-3 x 2-3 mm, circular or nearly so, compressed to subterete, glossy, light to dark reddish brown mottled with darker reddish brown, smooth, with circular marginal hilum concealed by rim-aril.

Notes: Herbaceous perennial of mountains from Texas to Arizona. *Cologania angustifolia* may hybridize with *C. pallida* Rose, the other United States species.

Colutea Linnaeus
Galegeae, Faboideae

Species: *arborescens* Linnaeus.

Common Names: Bladder-senna, bladderpod.

Seed 4.2-4.7 x 4-4.2 x 2 mm, mitten shaped, compressed, dull, dark reddish brown, smooth, with circular hilum in notch and concealed by whitish funicular remnant.

Notes: Shrub of Europe, occasionally cultivated and rarely escaped in eastern United States.

Coronilla Linnaeus
Coronilleae, Faboideae

Species: *varia* Linnaeus.

Common Names: Crown-vetch, axseed.

Seed 2.2-4 x 1-1.5 x 2 mm, oblong, compressed, semiglossy, reddish brown, with or without one longitudinal ridge on each face, with punctiform marginal hilum concealed by whitish funicular remnant and surrounded or not by dark eye. Loment (except apical) 5-8 x 1.5-3 x 1.5-3 mm, oblong with truncate ends (if apical, one end with long beak), terete, dull, buff to dirty brown, four-ribbed and reticulate.

Notes: Herbaceous perennial of Old World, cultivated and naturalized along roadsides from Maine to Minnesota and North Dakota, south to North Carolina and Oklahoma. Crown-vetch, an excellent soil conserving and ornamental plant, is used extensively on steep slopes and roadbanks of humid northern United States. Its agricultural value is limited because high tannin content reduces palatability and can be poisonous to nonruminants. Plants also recover slowly after mowing or grazing.

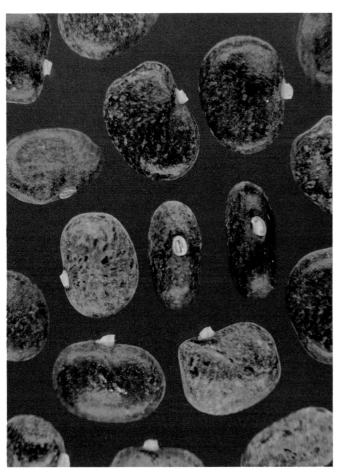

Clitoria ternatea 4.8X

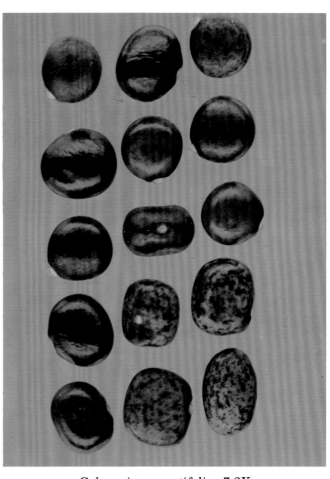

Cologania angustifolia 7.2X

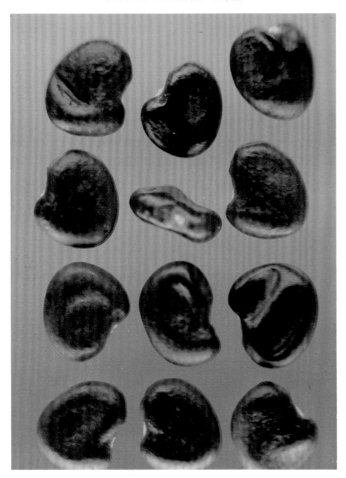

Colutea arborescens 6.4X

Coronilla varia 7.2X

Coursetia de Candolle
Robineae, Faboideae

Species: *microphylla* A. Gray
Common Name: Baby bonnett.
Seed 3.5-5 x 3-4 x 2 mm, circular or nearly so, compressed, glossy, reddish brown, smooth, with circular marginal hilum partially concealed or not by whitish funicular remnant.
Notes: Shrub of dry rocky slopes and canyons of Arizona. The correct name may be *Coursetia glandulosa* A. Gray.

Cracca Bentham
Robinieae, Faboideae

Species: *caribaea* (Jacquin) Bentham.
Common Name: Cracca.
Seed 2-3 x 1.8-2.3 x 1 mm, oblong to square, compressed, dull, reddish brown mottled with brown, smooth, with circular marginal hilum with or without tongue-aril.
Notes: Herbaceous perennial of rocky slopes often with live oaks in Cochise, Santa Cruz, and Pima Counties, Arizona. Previously known in U.S. floras as *Cracca edwardsii* A. Gray.

Crotalaria Linnaeus
Crotalarieae, Faboideae

Species: *pallida* Aiton.
Common Names: Striped crotalaria, smooth crotalaria.
Seed 3-3.5 x 2.2-2.5 x 2 mm, mitten shaped, compressed, glossy, tan to reddish brown faintly streaked with darker brown, smooth, with circular hilum in notch.
Notes: Herbaceous annual of the tropics, cultivated primarily as a cover and green manure crop in the southeastern United States, especially well adapted to sandy soils of coastal plains. Coarse stalks make hay of low palatability, but forage is not poisonous as it is in *C. spectabalis*. Striped crotalaria is known as either *C. mucronata* Desvaux or *C. striata* de Candolle in U.S. floras, but Polhill (1982) treats both as synonyms of *C. pallida*.

Crotalaria Linnaeus
Crotalarieae, Faboideae

Species: *sagittalis* Linnaeus.
Common Name: Rattlebox.
Seed 2-2.5 x 2-2.2 x 1 mm, mitten shaped, compressed, glossy, tan to brown or reddish brown, smooth, with circular hilum in notch and surrounded by collar.
Notes: Herbaceous annual in dry waste areas from Massachusetts to Minnesota, south to Florida, Nebraska and Texas.

Coursetia microphylla 7.2X

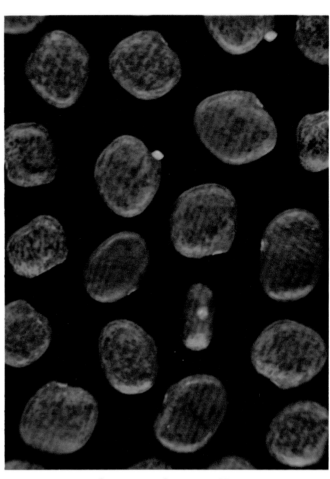

Cracca caribaea 8.8X

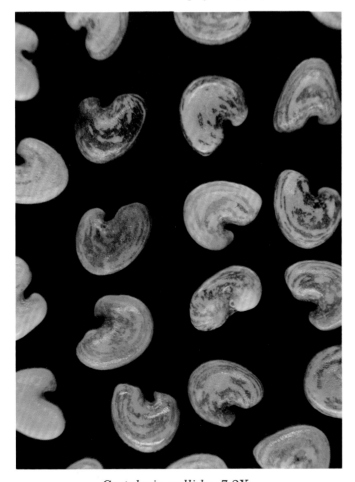

Crotalaria pallida 7.2X

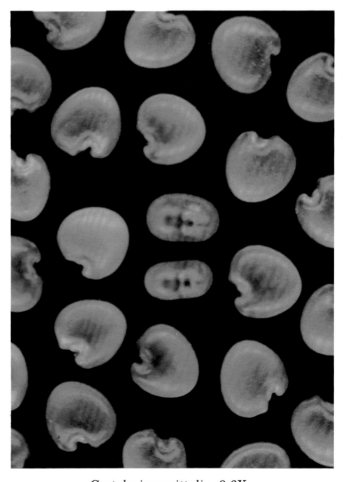

Crotalaria sagittalis 9.6X

43

Crotalaria Linnaeus
Crotalarieae, Faboideae

Species: *spectabilis* Roth.

Common Name: Showy crotalaria.

Seed 4.8-5 x 3.4-3.7 x 2 mm, mitten shaped, compressed, glossy, blackish green to blackish brown, smooth, with oblong hilum in notch and occluded by radicle lobe.

Notes: Herbaceous annual of Old World tropics, naturalized along roadsides and waste places from Virginia to Missouri, south to Florida and Texas. Showy crotalaria is cultivated in southeastern states as a summer annual cover and green manure crop and is especially adapted to sandy soils of coastal plains. Showy crotalaria contains monocrotaline which may kill livestock.

Cyamopsis de Candolle
Indigofereae, Faboideae

Species: *tetragonoloba* (Linnaeus) Taubert.

Common Names: Guar, cluster-bean.

Seed 5-5.3 x 4.3-4.7 x 2.8-3 mm, square, compressed, dull, light tan to blackish brown, tuberculate, with elliptic marginal hilum concealed by whitish funicular remnant.

Notes: Herbaceous annual of India, cultivated as green manure crop in Arizona, California and Texas and grown for seed in southern Oklahoma and northern Texas. Except for sheep, livestock refuse to graze guar because of its hard, bristly hairs. Seed are used for livestock feed and as a source of mucilage, which can be used as a substitute for *Ceratonia siliqua* in the manufacture of paper. Young pods may be eaten like *Phaseolus vulgaris,* mature pods cooked like a vegetable, and mature seeds used like *Lens culinaris.* Young leaves are a spinach substitute (Duke, 1981). Previously known as *Cyamopsis psoralioides* DC.

Cytisus Willdenow
Genisteae Faboideae

Species: *scoparius* (Linnaeus) Link.

Common Name: Scotch broom.

Seed 3-4 x 2-2.7 x 2 mm, somewhat mitten shaped, compressed, glossy, reddish to yellowish brown, smooth, with circular marginal hilum usually partially concealed by rim-aril.

Notes: Shrub of Europe, naturalized in dry soils and cultivated to a limited extent as an ornamental from Nova Scotia to Georgia and Alabama, and from Washington to California.

Dalbergia Linnaeus f.
Dalbergieae, Faboideae

Species: *sissoo* Roxburg ex de Candolle.

Common Name: Dalbergia.

Seed 7.5-8.2 x 5-5.2 x 2 mm, oblong, flattened, semiglossy, reddish brown, smooth, with punctiform marginal hilum subtended by dark raphe and lens. One-seeded indehiscent fruit 40-45 x 10-15 x 2 mm, elliptic, flattened, dull, tan, reticulate.

Notes: Tree of India, cultivated and naturalized in south Florida.

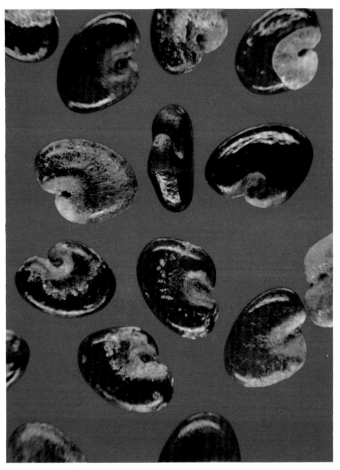

Crotalaria spectabilis 7.2X

Cyamopsis tetragonoloba 4.8X

Cytisus scoparius 9.6X

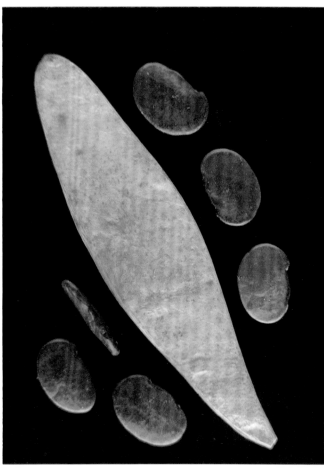

Dalbergia sissoo 3.2X

45

Dalea Lucanus
Amorpheae, Faboideae

Species: *leporina* (Aiton) A. A. Bullock.

Common Name: Indigo bush.

Seed 1.5-1.8 x 1.5-1.6 x 1 mm, mitten shaped, compressed, glossy, greenish brown to reddish brown, smooth, with circular marginal hilum surrounded by lighter color halo. One-seeded indehiscent fruit, concealed in silvery pubescent indurate calyx, 2 x 2 x 1 mm, mitten shaped, compressed, dull, gray, glandularly dotted.

Notes: Herbaceous annual becoming weedy in fields and along streambanks, shores, and highways from Minnesota to North Dakota, south to Indiana, Missouri, Texas and New Mexico.

Dalea Lucanus
Amorpheae, Faboideae

Species: *purpurea* Ventenat.

Common Name: Purple prairie-clover.

Seed 1.6-2 x 1.3-1.8 x 1-1.5 mm, mitten shaped, compressed, glossy, reddish tan to tan, smooth, with punctiform marginal hilum. One-seeded indehiscent fruit concealed by golden pubescent indurate calyx usually with filaments and style, 2-2.5 x 1-1.5, x 1 mm, subcircular, compressed to subterete, dull, reddish brown to golden, with upper one-half covered by golden hairs.

Notes: Herbaceous perennial of prairies, shores, and sandy areas from Saskatchewan to Alberta, south to Illinois and Kentucky and discontinuously to Alabama and Louisiana, west to Oklahoma and New Mexico. Two varieties are recognized in the United States: Var. *arenicola* (Wemple) Barneby and var. *purpurea.* Purple prairie-clover is known in most U.S. floras as *Petalostemon purpureum* (Ventenat) Rydberg.

Daviesia Smith
Mirbelieae, Faboideae

Species: *horrida* Meissner.

Common Name: Bitter-pea.

Seed 4.2-4.5 x 2.4-2.8 x 2 mm, oblong, compressed, semiglossy, reddish brown usually mottled with black and for some seed mottles coalesce making seed almost entirely black, smooth, with oblong marginal hilum partially concealed by honey-colored rim-aril. Previously known as *Daviesia latifolia.*

Notes: Shrub or subshrub of Australia, cultivated in California.

Delonix Rafinesque
Caesalpinieae, Caesalpinioideae

Species: *regia* (Bojer ex Hooker) Rafinesque.

Common Name: Royal poinciana.

Seed 19-21 x 6-7.5 x 5 mm, oblong, compressed, dull, ochre mottled and streaked with reddish brown to brown and encircled by darker colored margin, with concentric fracture lines (best seen in center of faces), with punctiform subapical hilum concealed or not by funicular remnant.

Notes: Tree of Madagascar, cultivated in Florida.

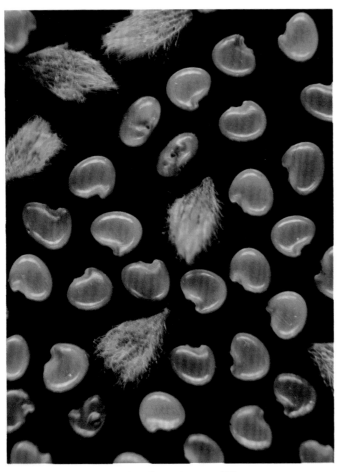

Dalea leporina 7.2X

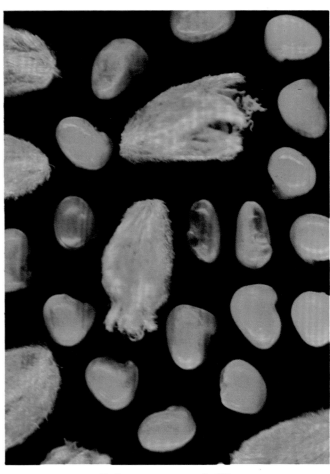

Dalea purpurea 9.6X

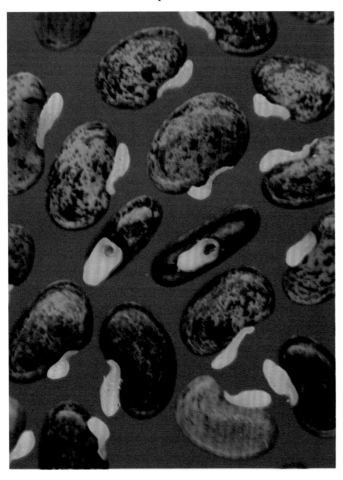

Daviesia horrida 8.0X

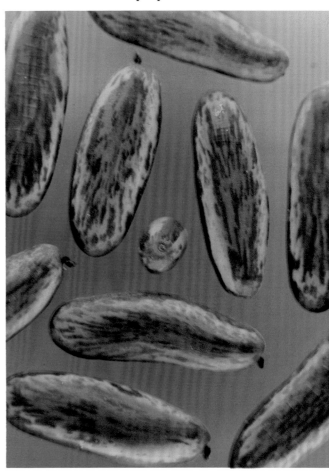

Delonix regia 3.2X

47

Desmanthus Willdenow
Mimoseae, Mimosoideae
Species: *illinoensis* (Michaux) Macmillian ex Robinson & Fernald.
Common Names: Prairie-mimosa, prickleweed.
Seed 3.8-5 x 2.5-3 x 1 mm, ovate, flattened, semiglossy, reddish brown with or without golden patches caused by raised cuticle, with 90% pleurogram on each face, with punctiform subapical hilum.
Notes: Herbaceous perennial along margins of woods and streambanks and in disturbed areas and grasslands from Pennsylvania to North Dakota, south to Florida and New Mexico.

Desmanthus Willdenow
Mimoseae, Mimosoideae
Species: *leptolobus* Torrey & Gray.
Common Name: Prairie-mimosa.
Seed 3.5-4 x 1.7-2.3 x 1-1.5 mm, oblong, compressed, glossy, reddish brown, with 90% pleurogram on each face, and punctiform subapical hilum.
Notes: Herbaceous perennial of disturbed areas and prairies from Kansas to Texas.

Desmodium Desvaux
Desmodieae, Faboideae
Species: *canadense* (Linnaeus) de Candolle.
Common Names: Hoary tickclover, tick-trefoil, sticktight.
Seed 2.8-3.5 x 2-2.2 x 1 mm, C- or D-shaped, compressed, glossy, reddish brown, smooth, with circular marginal hilum surrounded by light colored collar. One-seeded loment 5-6 x 4-5 x 2 mm, triangular, flattened, dull, brown, with short brown apically-hooked hairs, reticulate.
Notes: Herbaceous perennial of open woods and prairies from Nova Scotia to Saskatchewan, south to Virginia, Ohio River basin, Missouri and Oklahoma.

Desmodium Desvaux
Desmodieae, Faboideae
Species: *glutinosum* (Muhlenberg ex Willdenow) Wood.
Common Names: Tick-trefoil, sticktight.
Seed 7-8.5 x 4-5 x 1 mm, falcate, flattened, semiglossy, reddish brown, rugose, with circular marginal hilum concealed by whitish funicular remnant and surrounded by black eye and with black raphe between hilum and lens. Loment 9-11 x 5-6 x 2 mm, D-shaped, flattened, dull, reddish brown, with short apically-hooked hairs, reticulate.
Notes: Herbaceous perennial in woods from Nova Scotia to Saskatchewan, south to Georgia and Texas.

Desmanthus illinoensis 7.2X

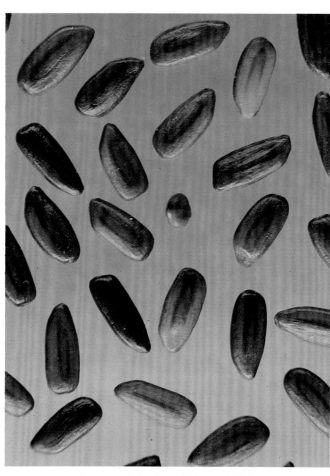

Desmanthus leptolobus 4.8X

Desmodium canadense 7.2X

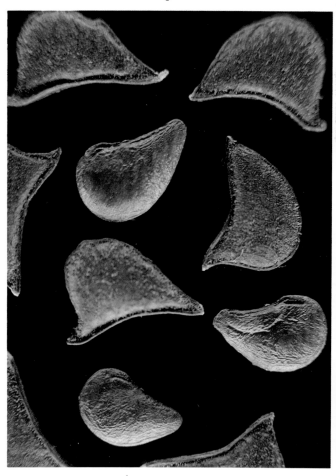

Desmodium glutinosum 4.4X

Desmodium Desvaux
Desmodieae, Faboideae

Species: *tortuosum* (Swartz) de Candolle.

Common Name: Florida beggarweed.

Seed 2.3-2.7 x 1.7-2 x 1 mm, irregularly oblong to ovate, flattened, glossy, reddish brown, smooth, with circular marginal hilum surrounded by collar of same color as seed coat and darker colored incomplete eye. Loment 3.5-5 x 2.5-3 x 1.5 mm, nearly circular, flattened, dull, brown, with short apically-hooked hairs and reticulate.

Notes: Herbaceous annual of South America, cultivated and naturalized (becoming weedy) from Florida to Mississippi. A few hectares of Florida beggarweed are grown on the southeastern coastal plains for pasture, hay, green manure, and quail feed. Previously known as *Desmodium purpureum* de Candolle.

Dichrostachys (de Candolle) Wight & Arnott
Mimoseae, Mimosoideae

Species: *cinerea* (Linnaeus) Wight & Arnott.

Common Name: Dichrostachys.

Seed 4-6 x 3.5-5 x 2 mm, ovate, compressed, glossy, reddish brown, with 90% pleurogram on each face and punctiform apical hilum.

Notes: Thorny shrub to small tree of Africa and India, naturalized in Florida and cultivated in California.

Dioclea Kunth
Diocleinae, Phaseoleae, Faboideae

Species: *multiflora* (Torrey & Gray) C. Mohr.

Common Name: Dioclea.

Seed 6.8-7.5 x 5-7 x 5-5.5 mm, oblong, compressed, dull, dark reddish brown streaked with bright reddish brown, smooth, with oblong marginal hilum surrounded by rim-aril.

Notes: Herbaceous perennial vine in alluvial woods from Kentucky to Florida, west to Arkansas and Texas.

Dioclea Kunth
Diocleinae, Phaseoleae, Faboideae

Species: *reflexa* Hooker f.

Common Name: Sea purse.

Seed 25-33 x 20-27 x 13-18 mm, subcircular to oblong, compressed, glossy, reddish brown mottled and streaked with black which may coalesce making seeds nearly black, rugose, with linear hilum occupying about three-quarters of seed circumference.

Notes: Sea purse is a woody vine of New World tropics, apparently not present in the United States. Seeds regularly reach Gulf and Atlantic beaches (Gunn, Dennis, and Paradine, 1976). The correct name may be *Dioclea hexandra* (Ralph) Mabberley.

Desmodium tortuosum 9.6X

Dichrostachys cinerea 7.2X

Dioclea multiflora 3.2X

Dioclea reflexa 1.4X

51

Diphysa Jacquin
Robinieae, Faboideae

Species: *thurberi* (A. Gray) Rydberg.

Common Name: Diphysa.

Seed 6.5-7 x 4.5 x 3 mm, oblong, compressed, semiglossy, reddish brown, smooth, with elliptic marginal hilum partially concealed by whitish funicular remnant and surrounded by collar of same color as seed coat.

Notes: Shrub of Huachuca Mountains of southeastern Arizona. Only two seeds were studied.

Dipteryx Schreber
Dipteryxeae, Faboideae

Species: *odorata* (Aublet) Willdenow.

Common Name: Tonka-bean.

Seed 40-50 x 13-15 x 8-10 mm, oblong, compressed, dull, blackish brown, rugose, with punctiform marginal hilum. One-seeded indehiscent fruit 60-70 x 30-60 x 30-60 mm, oblong, terete, dull, brown to yellowish brown, rugose.

Notes: Tree which is not present in the United States. Tonka-bean was selected to represent the three-genus tribe Dipteryxeae of Central and South America. Tonka-bean seeds are a commercial source of coumarin used as a fragrance in tobacco, foodstuffs, soaps, etc. (Duke, 1981).

Entada Adanson
Mimoseae, Mimosoideae

Species: *gigas* (Linnaeus) Fawcett & Rendle.

Common Name: Sea heart.

Seed 45-80 x 44-70 x 15-20 mm, oblong to cordate, compressed, glossy, dark brown, with reticulate fracture lines and circular apical hilum.

Notes: Sea heart is a woody vine of New World tropics, apparently not present in the United States. Seeds regularly reach Gulf and Atlantic beaches (Gunn, Dennis, and Paradine, 1976).

Enterolobium Martius
Ingeae, Mimosoideae

Species: *cyclocarpum* (Jacquin) Grisebach.

Common Name: Large earpod.

Seed 20 x 15 x 8 mm, ovate, compressed, dull, reddish brown, with 100% pleurogram marked with yellowish band on each face and punctiform apical hilum concealed or not by whitish funicule.

Notes: Tree of tropical America, cultivated in Florida and perhaps other southern states.

Diphysa thurberi 6.4X

Dipteryx odorata .96X

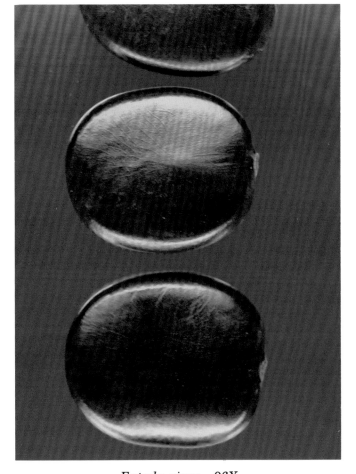

Entada gigas .96X

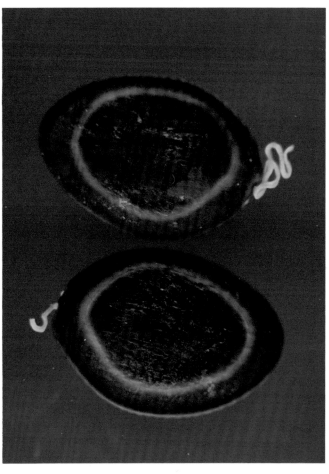

Enterolobium cyclocarpum 3.2X

Errazurizia Philippi
Amorpheae, Faboideae

Species: *rotunda* (Wooton) Barneby.

Common Name: Errazurizia.

Seed 4.6-7 x 2.7-3.7 x 2-2.5 mm, oblong, compressed, glossy, reddish brown, with shiny patches caused by exudates from fruit glands, with circular marginal hilum subtended by grooved raphe. One-seeded indehiscent fruit 8-10 x 5-5.4 x 2 mm, elliptic, compressed, dull, reddish tan, with short white hairs and dark reddish brown glands, subtended by calyx with short white hairs and brown glands.

Notes: Small shrub of rimrock and ledges of Arizona. "Known only from two small areas on creeks flowing to the Little Colorado River in Coconino and Navajo counties" (Barneby, 1977). Plants may become engulfed in drifting sand.

Erythrina Linnaeus
Erythrininae, Phaseoleae, Faboideae

Species: *crista-galli* Linnaeus.

Common Name: Seibo.

Seed 11-15 x 7-8 x 6-7 mm, oblong, terete, semiglossy, dark reddish brown streaked with bright reddish brown, smooth, with oblong marginal hilum concealed by funicular remnant and surrounded by rim-aril.

Notes: Tree of southern South America, cultivated at least in Texas. Seibo is the national flower of Argentina.

Erythrina Linnaeus
Erythrininae, Phaseoleae, Faboideae

Species: *herbacea* Linnaeus.

Common Names: Coral-bean, eastern coral-bean, cardinal spear.

Seed 10-11 x 6-7 x 6-7 mm, elliptic, terete, glossy, red, smooth, with elliptic marginal hilum and partial rim-aril.

Notes: Thorny herbaceous perennial to shrub or small tree of open sandy woods and clearings along coast from North Carolina to Texas.

Euchresta J. J. Bennett
Euchresteae, Faboideae

Species: *japonica* Hooker f. ex Regel.

Common Name: Euchresta.

Seed 15-18 x 9-10 x 6-7 mm, oblong, compressed, glossy, reddish black to black rugose, with circular apical hilum.

Notes: Shrub not present in the United States. Selected to represent the monotypic tribe Euchresteae of Japan and China. For additional information see Ohashi (1978). Previously known as *Euchresta trifoliata* Merrill.

Errazurizia rotunda 6.4X

Erythrina crista-galli 3.2X

Erythrina herbacea 3.2X

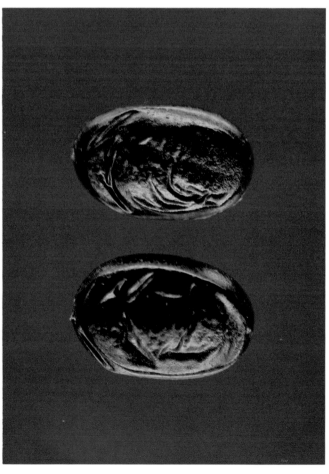

Euchresta japonica 3.2X

Eysenhardtia Kunth
Amorpheae, Faboideae

Species: *texana* Scheele.

Common Name: Kidneywood.

Seed 3-4 x 1.3-1.5 x 1 mm, falcate, compressed, semiglossy, black to brown or tan, smooth, with punctiform marginal hilum surrounded by whitish collar. One-seeded indehiscent fruit 6-9 x 2-2.5 x 1 mm, falcate, compressed, dull, dusty brown, glandularly dotted, reticulate, with or without calyx.

Notes: Shrub of calcareous soils of southern Texas.

Galactia P. Browne
Diocleinae, Phaseoleae, Faboideae

Species: *volubilis* (Linnaeus) Britton.

Common Name: Milk-pea.

Seed 3.5-4.3 x 2.5-3 x 2 mm, oblong, compressed, dull, reddish brown to tan and mottled or not with black, smooth, with oblong marginal hilum with rim- to tongue-aril and surrounded by black eye.

Notes: Herbaceous perennial vine of upland woods from New York southwest to Kentucky, Missouri, Oklahoma, south to Florida and Texas. Two varieties are recognized in the United States: Var. *mississippiensis* (Vail) Rydberg and var. *volubilis*.

Galega Linnaeus
Galegeae, Faboideae

Species: *officinalis* Linnaeus.

Common Names: Goatsrue, galega.

Seed 3.5-4.5 x 1.5-2 x 1.5 mm, oblong with one margin notched, compressed, dull, reddish to greenish tan or tan, minutely tuberculate, with circular marginal hilum surrounded by funicular remnant ring.

Notes: Herbaceous perennial of Europe, naturalized along irrigation ditches in Utah. Goatsrue is an escaped plant introduction that has become a federal noxious weed.

Genista Linnaeus
Genistieae, Faboideae

Species: *tinctoria* Linnaeus.

Common Names: Dyer's greenwood, common woadaxen, whin.

Seed 2-3 x 2-2.5 x 1 mm, subcircular, compressed, glossy, reddish brown to tan, smooth, with circular marginal hilum usually with rim-aril.

Notes: Shrub of Europe, cultivated and naturalized in New England, New York and Virginia.

Eysenhardtia texana 6.4X

Galactia volubilis 7.2X

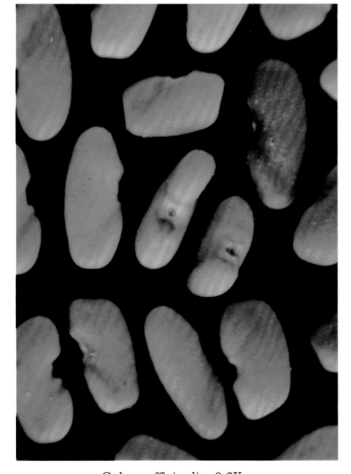

Galega officinalis 9.6X

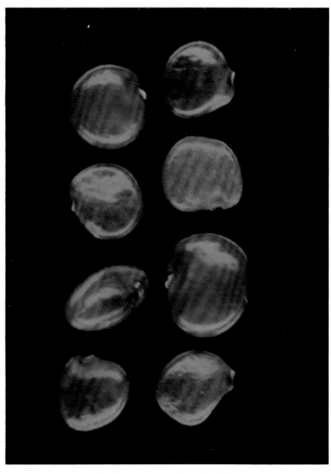

Genista tinctoria 9.6X

Genistidium I. M. Johnston
Robineae, Faboideae

Species: *dumosum* I. M. Johnston.

Common Name: Genistidium.

Seed 4.2 x 3.5 x 2 mm, circular, compressed, semiglossy, reddish brown mottled with black, smooth, with circular marginal hilum with rim-aril.

Notes: Shrub of very dry limestone hills in Texas. The rarest native United States legume. Only one or two plants have been found in south Brewster County and one plant in Coahuila, Mexico. Only one seed was obtained and studied.

Gleditsia Linnaeus
Caesalpinieae, Caesalpinioideae

Species: *aquatica* Marshall.

Common Name: Water-locust.

Seed 10-12 x 9-11 x 3 mm, subcircular, flattened, semiglossy, brown, with concentric fracture lines and punctiform apical hilum concealed by whitish funicular remnant.

Notes: Tree of flood plains from Maryland to Missouri, and south to Florida and Texas. Locally cultivated within and beyond its natural range.

Gleditsia Linnaeus
Caesalpinieae, Caesalpinioideae

Species: *triacanthos* Linnaeus.

Common Names: Honey-locust, honey shuck.

Seed 9-10 x 6.5-7 x 5 mm, oblong, compressed, glossy, brown, with concentric and reticulate fracture lines and punctiform subapical hilum.

Notes: Tree of bottomland and upland pastures of the United States except northern New England and several western States. Several cultivars are available and these as well as wild trees are planted.

Glottidium Desvaux
Robineae, Faboideae

Species: *vesicaria* (Jacquin) C. Mohr.

Common Names: Bladder pod, bagpod.

Seed 11-12 x 5.5-6.5 x 5-6 mm, oblong, subterete, semiglossy, reddish brown, with or without brown patches caused by raised cuticle, with oblong marginal hilum surrounded by lighter colored collar.

Notes: Herbaceous annual of ditches and low fields of coastal plains from North Carolina to Texas. Known in some U.S. floras as *Sesbania vesicaria* (Jacquin) Elliott.

Genistidium dumosum 9.6X

Gleditsia aquatica 3.2X

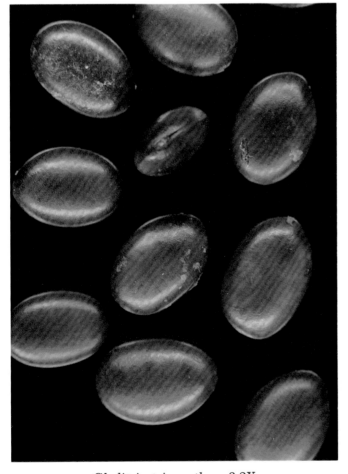

Gleditsia triacanthos 3.2X

Glottidium vesicaria 3.2X

Glycine Willldenow
Glycininae, Phaseoleae, Faboideae
Species: *max* (Linnaeus) Merrill.
Common Name: Soybean.
Seed 4-9 x 3-8 x 3-7 mm, circular to oblong, compressed to subterete, semiglossy, variously colored (buff, greenish yellow, reddish brown, black to black mottled with buff), smooth, with oblong marginal hilum and tongue-aril (may be knocked off) and if buff to greenish yellow surrounded or not by brownish to blackish eye.
Notes: Herbaceous annual of Asia, widely cultivated in the United States, and second only to corn in the number of hectares and cash value. Soybean is intensely cultivated from northern Ohio west to central Minnesota, south to the Mississippi River Delta. The purple color on some buff to greenish yellow seed is caused by the fungus *Cercospora kikuchii* M. W. Gardner.

Glycyrrhiza Linnaeus
Galegeae, Faboideae
Species: *lepidota* (Nuttall) Pursh.
Common Names: Wild licorice, devil's shoestring, sweet root.
Seed 2.5-3.5 x 2-2.5 x 2 mm, oblong to irregular, compressed, semiglossy, reddish to greenish brown, smooth, with circular marginal hilum partially concealed by whitish funicular ring. One-seeded indehiscent fruit 12-15 x 4-5 x 3-4 mm (excluding spines), oblong, compressed, dull, reddish brown, with numerous hooked spines.
Notes: Herbaceous perennial of moist prairies from Ontario to Alberta and Washington, south to Arkansas, Texas and California. Wild licorice may become a serious weed. Two varieties are recognized in the United States: Var. *glutinosa* (Nuttall) Watson of the far west and var. *lepidota* of the remainder of the range. Both varieties have some of the properties of the licorice of commerce, *G. glabra* Linnaeus.

Gymnocladus Lamarck
Caesalpinieae, Caesalpinioideae
Species: *dioica* (Linnaeus) Koch.
Common Name: Kentucky coffeetree.
Seed 15-18 x 14-15 x 10-12 mm, subcircular, compressed, glossy to dull, dark brown, with reticulate fracture lines and punctiform apical hilum concealed by funicular remnant.
Notes: Tree of bottomland on north-facing slopes from New Hampshire to South Dakota, south to Georgia and Oklahoma. Kentucky coffeetree is cultivated for timber and fence posts and to a lesser degree as an ornamental within and beyond its native range.

Haematoxylum Linnaeus
Caesalpinieae, Caesalpinioideae
Species: *campechianum* Linnaeus.
Common Name: Logwood.
Seed 8-12 x 3 x 1 mm, oblong, flattened, semiglossy, brown with lighter colored band on center of each face, smooth, with punctiform marginal hilum concealed by tan, funicular remnant. One- to three-seeded indehiscent fruit 20-40 x 8-12 x 10 mm, oblong to lanceolate, compressed, dull, tan, with each face bearing longitudinal line of weakness (not a suture) which separates allowing seeds to fall.
Notes: Spiny shrub to tree of tropical America, cultivated in subtropical Florida. The biological stain haematoxylon is produced from the wood.

Glycine max 3.2X

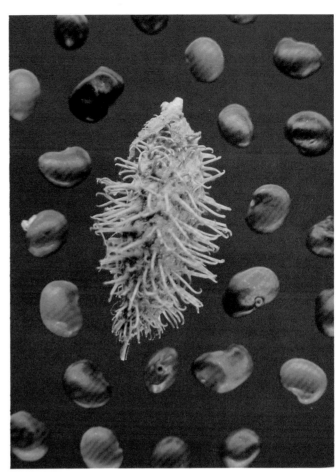

Glycyrrhiza lepidota 4.8X

Gymnocladus dioica 3.2X

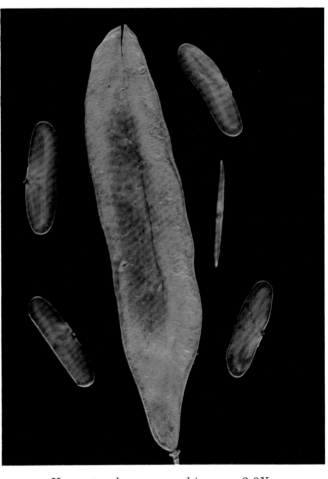

Haematoxylum campechianum 2.8X

Hedysarum Linnaeus
Hedysareae, Faboideae

Species: *alpinum* Linnaeus var. *americanum* Michaux.

Common Name: Sweet-vetch.

Seed 3.5-4 x 3 x 2 mm, oblong with prominent radicle lobe, compressed, dull, dark reddish brown, smooth, with circular marginal hilum partially concealed by funicular ring. Loment 5-11 x 5-7 x 2 mm, oblong to ovate, flattened, dull, tan, with or without short hairs, reticulate.

Notes: Herbaceous perennial of Eurasia, naturalized along river banks, hills, and ledges of Newfoundland to Maine, Vermont and Quebec, and Manitoba to British Columbia. Plants of western Canada are recognized as var. *americanum*.

Hoffmannseggia Cavanilles
Caesalpinieae, Caesalpinioideae

Species: *glauca* (Ortega) Eifert.

Common Names: Pignut, hog-potato, rushpea.

Seed 3.2-3.7 x 2.2-2.5 x 2 mm, ovate, compressed, semiglossy, brown, with golden patches or "dust" caused by raised cuticle, with punctiform subapical hilum concealed by funicular remnant.

Notes: Herbaceous perennial of disturbed soil from Kansas to California, south to Mexico. This species, native to both North and South America, has weedy tendencies. Previously known as *Hoffmannseggia densiflora* Bentham.

Hymenaea Linnaeus
Detarieae, Caesalpinioideae

Species: *courbaril* Linnaeus.

Common Name: West Indian-locust.

Seed 20-30 x 15-20 x 10-15 mm, oblong, compressed, dull, dark brown, with or without tan scurfy endocarp in patches or concealing entire seed, with punctiform subapical hilum.

Notes: Tree not present in the United States. Selected to represent the large tropical tribe Detarieae primarily of Africa and secondarily of South America. West Indian-locust is a New World tree whose indehiscent fruits drift to Gulf and Atlantic beaches (Gunn, Dennis, and Paradine, 1976).

Hypocalyptus Thunberg
Liparieae, Faboideae

Species: *sophorides* (Bergius) Baillon.

Common Name: Hypocalyptus.

Seed 4-4.5 x 3-3.3 x 2.7-3 mm, oblong, subterete, semiglossy, medium to dark brown, faintly rugose, with oblong marginal hilum and prominent whitish rim-aril.

Notes: Shrub to small tree not present in the United States. It was selected to represent the five-genus tribe Liparieae of South Africa.

Hedysarum alpinum var. americanum 6.4X

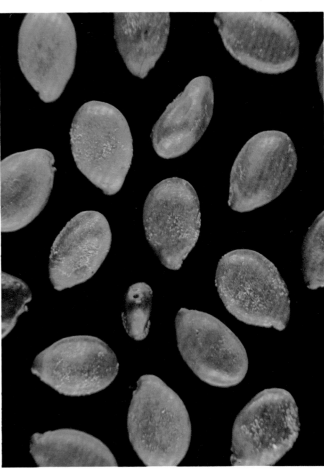

Hoffmannseggia glauca 7.2X

Hymenaea courbaril 3.2X

Hypocalyptus sophorides 6.4X

63

Indigofera Linnaeus
Indigofereae, Faboideae

Species: *hirsuta* Linnaeus.
Common Name: Hairy indigo.
Seed 1.5-1.7 x 1.1-1.3 x 1.1-1.3 mm, square in outline and transection, dull, grayish, pitted, with elliptic marginal hilum.
Notes: Herbaceous annual of tropical Africa, naturalized along roadsides and in waste places of south Florida where it was introduced as a crop.

Kennedia Ventenat
Kennediinae, Phaseoleae, Faboideae

Species: *rubicunda* Ventenat.
Common Name: Dusky coral-pea.
Seed 4.5-5 x 3-4 x 2-2.5 mm, oblong, compressed, glossy, reddish to yellowish brown with or without brown mottling, smooth, with oblong marginal hilum partially concealed by honey-colored rim-aril.
Notes: Herbaceous perennial vine not present in the United States. It was selected to represent the subtribe Kennediinae with three genera of Australia and New Guinea.

Lablab Adanson
Phaseolinae, Phaseoleae, Faboideae

Species: *purpureus* Linnaeus.
Common Names: Hyacinth-bean, bonavist, Egyptian-bean.
Seed 10-13 x 7-9 x 6-7 mm, oblong, compressed, dull, yellowish tan to dark reddish brown, smooth, with linear marginal hilum concealed by whitish aril.
Notes: Herbaceous perennial vine (often treated as an annual) of Asia, cultivated in United States and naturalized in southern United States. Young pods and ripe seeds are edible, and seeds are sold in the flower seed packet trade. In U.S. floras the hyacinth-bean is known as *Dolichos lablab* Linnaeus. The correct name may be *Lablab nigra* Medikus.

Laburnum Fabricus
Genisteae, Faboideae

Species: *anagyroides* Medikus.
Common Names: Goldenchain or goldenchain tree, laburnum, bean-tree.
Seed 3-4.5 x 2.7-3.7 x 2.5-3 mm, oblong, with notch on one side, compressed, semiglossy, dark reddish brown, smooth, with circular marginal hilum with rim-aril.
Notes: Shrub to tree of southern Europe, cultivated as an ornamental and for wood production in northeastern United States. All plant parts are poisonous. Chewed and swallowed seeds and fruits can be fatal, and sucking on flowers is dangerous. Poison affects both humans and dogs.

Indigofera hirsuta 9.6X

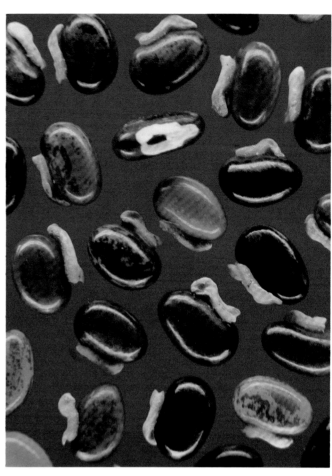

Kennedia rubicunda 4.8X

Lablab purpureus 3.2X

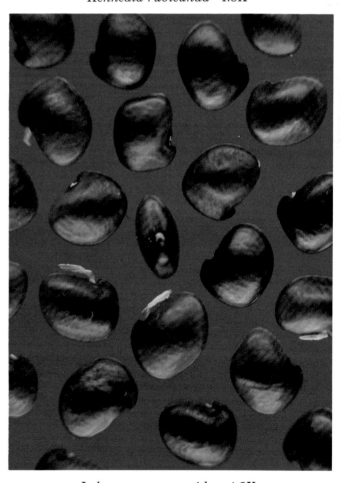

Laburnum anagyroides 4.8X

Lathyrus Linnaeus
Vicieae, Faboideae

Species: *hirsutus* Linnaeus.

Common Names: Caley-pea, rough-pea, wild winter-pea, singletary-pea.

Seed 3-4 x 3-3.5 x 3-3.5 mm, variously shaped (oblong, square, triangular), subterete to terete, dull, dark reddish brown, tuberculate, with wedge-shaped marginal hilum.

Notes: Herbaceous annual of southern Europe, naturalized along roadsides and in waste places from Virginia to Missouri, south to Georgia and Texas, and Oregon to California. Seeds cause lameness in cattle.

Lathyrus Linnaeus
Vicieae, Faboideae

Species: *latifolius* Linnaeus.

Common Names: Everlasting-pea, perennial sweet-pea.

Seed 3.5-5.5 x 2.7-4 x 2.7-4 mm, oblong to square, terete to square, dull, dark reddish brown, tuberculate, with linear marginal hilum.

Notes: Herbaceous perennial of Europe, naturalized along roadsides and in waste places from New England to Indiana and Missouri, south to Virginia, Oklahoma and Texas, and Washington to Arizona and Wyoming. Seeds are poisonous to livestock.

Lathyrus Linnaeus
Vicieae, Faboideae

Species: *odoratus* Linnaeus.

Common Names: Sweet-pea, annual sweet-pea, common sweet-pea.

Seed 4.5-5.5 x 4.5-5 x 4.5-5 mm, circular or nearly so, terete, dull, dark reddish brown, faintly rugose, with wedge-shaped marginal hilum.

Notes: Herbaceous annual of the Mediterranean region, cultivated throughout United States and escaped in waste places near the coast from Washington to California. Seeds are sold by the flower seed packet trade.

Lathyrus Linnaeus
Vicieae, Faboideae

Species: *sylvestris* Linnaeus.

Common Names: Flat-pea, Wagner-pea, everlasting-pea, perennial-pea.

Seed 4-6 x 4-4.5 x 4-4.5 mm, oblong to circular, terete, dull, dark reddish brown, rugose, with linear marginal hilum.

Notes: Herbaceous perennial of Europe, naturalized from Idaho to Washington and Oregon. Seeds are poisonous to livestock.

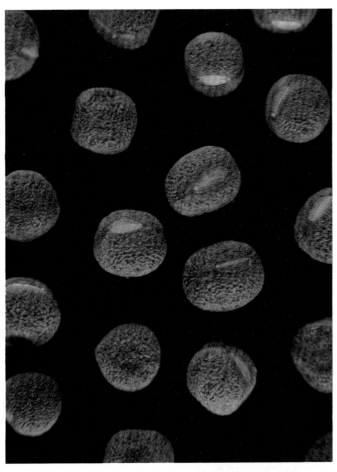

Lathyrus hirsutus 5.6X

Lathyrus latifolius 4.8X

Lathyrus odoratus 4.8X

Lathyrus sylvestris 5.6X

Lens Miller
Vicieae, Faboideae

Species: *culinaris* Medikus.

Common Name: Lentil.

Seed 4-7 x 4-7 x 2-3 mm, circular, compressed, dull because of gray bloom to glossy when bloom removed, reddish brown, smooth, with linear marginal hilum.

Notes: Herbaceous annual with tendrils of Europe and southwest Asia, cultivated in home gardens and commercially grown in Washington, Idaho, Oregon, and northern California. Lentil is grown for its edible seeds, mainly used in soups. Previously known as *Lens esculenta* Moench.

Lespedeza Michaux
Desmodieae, Faboideae

Species: *cuneata* (Dumont de Courset) G. Don.

Common Name: Sericea lespedeza.

Seed 1.8-2.4 x 1-1.3 x 0.8 mm, ovate, compressed, glossy, yellowish tan to reddish brown conspicuously to faintly mottled or not with purple, smooth, with punctiform marginal hilum partially concealed by funicular ring. One-seeded indehiscent fruit 3-4 x 1.8-2 x 2 mm, elliptic, compressed, semiglossy, reddish brown, reticulate, usually without calyx.

Notes: Subshrub of Asia, cultivated and naturalized from Maryland to Michigan, south to Virginia, Missouri, Oklahoma and Texas. Sericea lespedeza is used for forage, green manure, and as a cover crop especially on roadbanks. Cultivars with reduced tannic acid content are available.

Lespedeza Michaux
Desmodieae, Faboideae

Species: *stipulacea* Maximowicz.

Common Names: Korean lespedeza, Korean-clover, Korean bush-clover.

Seed 2-2.5 x 1.5-1.8 x 1 mm, oblong, compressed, semiglossy, dark to light reddish brown or tan, smooth, with punctiform marginal hilum surrounded by collar. One-seeded indehiscent fruit 3.5-4 x 2-2.5 x 1.5 mm, elliptic, compressed, dull, brown, with gray hairs and reticulate, usually three-quarters concealed by calyx.

Notes: Herbaceous annual of Asia, cultivated for forage and erosion control, and naturalized throughout eastern United States, south of Pennsylvania and Iowa.

Lespedeza Michaux
Desmodieae, Faboideae

Species: *striata* (Thunberg) Hooker & Arnott.

Common Names: Japanese lespedeza, common lespedeza, striate lespedeza, Japanese-clover, Japanese bush-clover.

Seed 1.7-2.3 x 1.2-1.7 x 1 mm, oblong, compressed, semiglossy, reddish brown, mottled to densely mottled with blackish purple, smooth, with punctiform marginal hilum surrounded by collar. One-seeded indehiscent fruit 3-4 x 2-3 x 1.5 mm, elliptic, compressed, dull, grayish brown, with gray hairs and reticulation and usually three-quarters concealed by calyx.

Notes: Herbaceous annual of Asia, cultivated for forage and green manure, used for soil erosion control, and naturalized throughout eastern United States south of Pennsylvania to Kansas.

Lens culinaris 4.8X

Lespedeza cuneata 9.6X

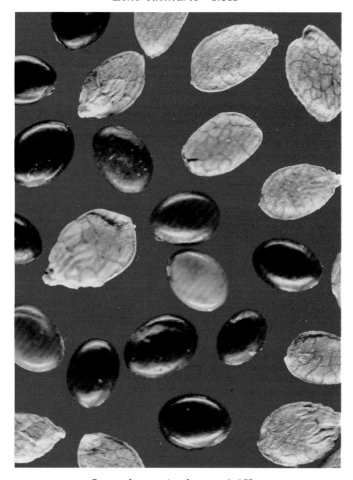

Lespedeza stipulacea 8.8X

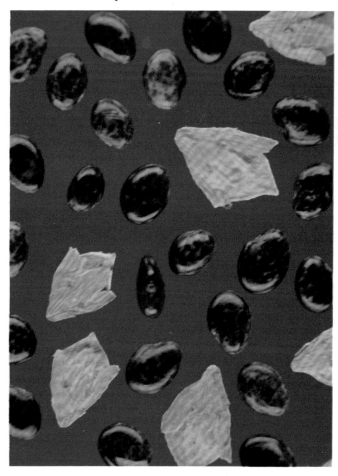

Lespedeza striata 8.8X

Lespedeza Michaux
Desmodieae, Faboideae

Species: *virginica* (Linnaeus) Britton.

Common Names: Virginia lespedeza, slender lespedeza.

Seed 1.5-2.5 x 1.2-1.5 x 1 mm, oblong, compressed, semiglossy, tan to brown, smooth, with punctiform marginal hilum surrounded by collar. One-seeded indehiscent fruit 3-6 x 2.2-3.5 x 1.5 mm, elliptic, compressed, dull, reddish brown, with gray hairs and reticulate and usually calyx absent.

Notes: Herbaceous perennial of dry upland woods and along roadsides from New England to Wisconsin and Kansas, south to Georgia and Texas. Virginia lespedeza has forage value and provides seeds for wild birds.

Leucaena Bentham
Mimoseae, Mimosoideae

Species: *leucocephala* (Lamarck) de Wit.

Common Names: Leucaena, jumbie-bean, lead-tree, popinac.

Seed 6-8 x 3.8-4.2 x 1.5-2 mm, oblong, compressed, glossy, brown, with 90% pleurogram on each face and inconspicuous reticulate fracture lines, with punctiform subapical hilum.

Notes: Shrub or small tree (but appearing like an herb) of New World origin, cultivated in Florida, Texas and California. Classified as a weed in some tropical countries, but cultivars with less weedy tendencies are available for cultivation.

Lonchocarpus Kunth
Millettieae, Faboideae

Species: *violaceus* Kunth.

Common Name: Purple lonchocarpus.

Seed 10-15 x 5.5-8.7 x 4-4.5 mm, C-shaped, compressed, semiglossy (often with glossy indehiscent fruit exudate), reddish brown, smooth, with wedge-shaped marginal hilum concealed by whitish funicular remnant.

Notes: Tree of the West Indies, naturalized on the Florida Keys.

Lotus Linnaeus
Loteae, Faboideae

Species: *corniculata* Linnaeus.

Common Name: Birdsfoot trefoil.

Seed 1.2-1.7 x 1-1.3 x 1 mm, oblong to mitten shaped, terete to compressed, semiglossy, brown to reddish brown with or without purple mottling, smooth, with punctiform marginal hilum partially concealed by funicular ring.

Notes: Herbaceous perennial of Europe and Asia, cultivated and naturalized primarily in northern United States and occurring throughout the United States except southeast Texas. Birdsfoot trefoil is primarily a pasture crop and is gaining popularity as a cover crop for road banks.

Lespedeza virginica 9.6X

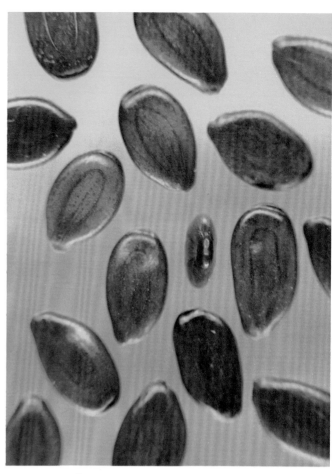

Leucanena leucocephala 4.8X

Lonchocarpus violaceus 3.2X

Lotus corniculata 9.6X

71

Lotus Linnaeus
Loteae, Faboideae

Species: *purshianus* (Bentham) Clements & Clements.

Common Name: Prairie trefoil.

Seed 2.5-3.5 x 1.2-2 x 1.2-2 mm, oblong, compressed to terete, glossy, reddish brown to tan mottled with black (both dense and diffuse mottles), smooth, with circular marginal hilum concealed by whitish funicular remnant.

Notes: Herbaceous annual of sandy or rocky areas from Virginia to Georgia and Tennessee, central United States, and western United States. Two varieties are recognized in United States: Var. *helleri* (Britton) Isely found in open areas of Virginia to Georgia and Tennessee, while var. *purshianus* is found in open areas west of the Mississippi River, except Colorado, New Mexico and Utah.

Lotus Linnaeus
Loteae, Faboideae

Species: *uliginosus* Schkuhr.

Common Name: Big trefoil.

Seed 0.8-1.1 x 0.7-0.9 x 0.7-0.9 mm, oblong to somewhat mitten shaped, terete, glossy, tan to brown or greenish, smooth, with circular marginal hilum concealed by whitish funicular ring.

Notes: Herbaceous perennial of Europe, cultivated in lowlands and naturalized in wet fields, sandy roadsides and ditches from Washington to California. Big trefoil shows promise as a pasture crop in southeastern coastal plains. It is known as *Lotus major* C. P. Smith in some U.S. floras.

Lupinus Linnaeus
Genisteae, Faboideae

Species: *albus* Linnaeus.

Common Names: White lupine, Egyptian lupine.

Seed 9-12 x 8-11 x 5-6 mm, square, compressed, semiglossy, ivory, faces often recessed, with elliptic hilum on one shoulder and surrounded by collar.

Notes: Herbaceous annual of Europe cultivated as green manure, pasture, or cover crop in southeastern coastal states. Unlike unimproved plants, newer cultivars do not have poisonous alkaloids concentrated in seeds and pods.

Lupinus Linnaeus
Genisteae, Faboideae

Species: *angustifolius* Linnaeus.

Common Name: Blue lupine.

Seed 5-9 x 4-6 x 4-6 mm, oblong, terete to compressed, semiglossy, gray mottled with ivory to brown or black and mottles may be dense or diffuse, smooth, with oblong hilum on one shoulder.

Notes: Herbaceous annual of Europe, cultivated as green manure, pasture, or cover crop in southeastern coastal states. Unlike unimproved plants, newer cultivars do not have poisonous alkaloids concentrated in seeds and pods.

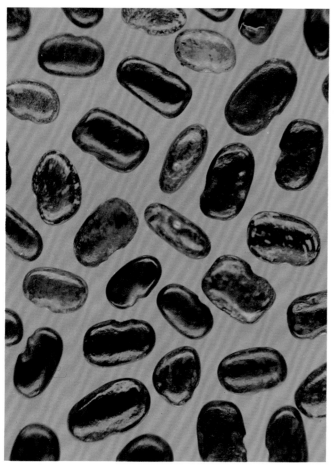

Lotus purshianus 7.2X

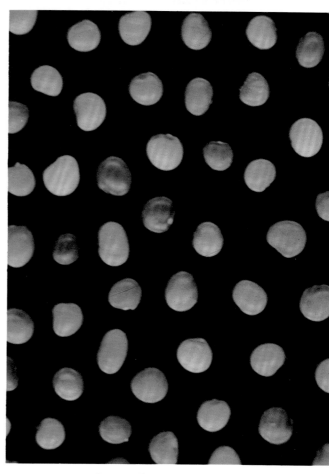

Lotus. uliginosus 9.6X

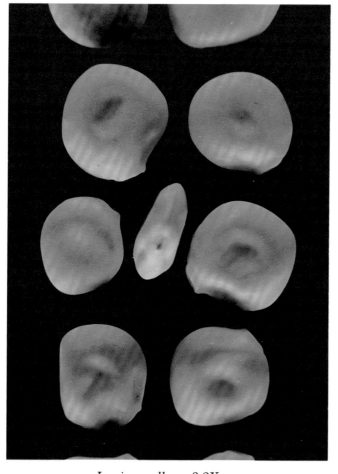

Lupinus albus 3.2X

Lupinus angustifolius 4.8X

Lupinus Linnaeus
Genisteae, Faboideae

Species: *chamissonis* Eschscholtz.
Common Name: Beach lupine.
Seed 5-5.7 x 3-4.5 x 2-3 mm, oblong, compressed, semiglossy, tan to brownish tan mottled or streaked with dark brown, smooth, with circular hilum on shoulder of seed and concealed or nearly so by whitish funicular remnant and surrounded by lighter colored collar.
Notes: Shrub of sandy beaches and dunes of southern California.

Lupinus Linnaeus
Genisteae, Faboideae

Species: *leucophyllus* Douglas ex Lindley.
Common Names: Western lupine, velvet lupine.
Seed 3.5-5 x 3-4 x 2-3 mm, oblong to square, compressed, glossy, tan to brown mottled or not with brown to dark brown, smooth, with circular hilum on shoulder of seed and partially concealed by funicular remnant and surrounded by lighter colored collar.
Notes: Herbaceous perennial of sagebrush scrub and yellow or ponderosa pine forests from Montana to Washington, south to Wyoming and California. Western lupine is poisonous to livestock and is a weedy species. Two varieties are recognized in the United States: Var. *leucophyllus* of New Mexico to California and var. *tenuispicus* C. P. Smith of Idaho, Oregon and Washington.

Lupinus Linnaeus
Genisteae, Faboideae

Species: *polyphyllus* Lindley.
Common Names: Large-leaved lupine, blue-pod lupine.
Seed 4.5-5.5 x 3.5-4 x 2-3 mm, oblong, compressed, glossy, brown to reddish brown mottled with darker brown to reddish brown, smooth, with elliptic hilum on shoulder of seed within lighter colored collar.
Notes: Herbaceous perennial of stream banks, meadows, moist forests from Alberta to British Columbia, south to Colorado and California. Two subspecies and one variety are recognized in the United States.

Lysiloma Bentham
Ingeae, Mimosoideae

Species: *sabicu* Bentham.
Common Name: Wild-tamarind.
Seed 5.5-9 x 4-5 x 1.5 mm, oblong, compressed, semiglossy to dull, dark reddish brown, with 90-100% pleurogram on each face and reticulate fracture lines mainly within areole, with punctiform subapical hilum.
Notes: Shrub or tree of the West Indies, cultivated in Florida. The tan sheen on photographed seeds is caused by partially raised cuticle.

Lupinus chamissonis 4.8X

Lupinus leucophyllus 6.4X

Lupinus polyphyllus 7.2X

Lysiloma sabicu 4.8X

Maackia Ruprecht & Maxomowicz
Sophoreae, Faboideae

Species: *amurensis* Ruprecht.

Common Name: Maackia.

Seed 6.5-9 x 3.5-4.5 x 3-3.5 mm, falcate, compressed, semiglossy, tan to reddish brown, smooth, with elliptic marginal hilum surrounded by a collar and subtended by prominent darker brown raphe.

Notes: Tree native of eastern Asia, cultivated in northern United States.

Macroptilium (Bentham) Urban
Phaseolinae, Phaseoleae, Faboideae

Species: *lathyroides* (Linnaeus) Urban.

Common Name: Annual siratro.

Seed 3-3.5 x 1.8-2.3 x 1.5-2 mm, oblong, subterete, semiglossy, reddish brown mottled and streaked with darker and lighter reddish brown and black, smooth, with wedge-shaped marginal hilum concealed by tannish funicular remnant.

Notes: Herbaceous perennial (annual in cultivation) of the American tropics and subtropics, escaping from cultivation in southern Florida. Referred to in U.S. floras as *Phaseolus lathyroides* Linnaeus.

Marina Liebmann
Amorpheae, Faboideae

Species: *parryi* (Torrey & Gray) Barneby.

Common Name: Parry marina.

Seed 1.7-2 x 1.4-1.6 x 1 mm, mitten shaped, compressed, glossy, reddish to greenish brown, smooth, with punctiform hilum in notch and surrounded by tan collar. One-seeded indehiscent fruit, nearly concealed by reddish brown glandular calyx covered by white hairs, 2-2.5 x 1.5-2 x 1.5 mm, D-shaped, compressed, dull, greenish to reddish brown, two parted (upper two-thirds bearing large light to dark reddish-brown glands and white hairs and lower one-third translucent and without glands and hairs).

Notes: Herbaceous perennial of rocky or sandy outwash fans, washes and hillsides from Colorado to Arizona and California.

Medicago Linnaeus
Trifolieae, Faboideae

Species: *arabica* (Linnaeus) Hudson.

Common Names: Spotted medick, spotted or southern burclover.

Seed 2.5-3 x 1.3-1.6 x 1 mm, C-shaped, compressed, semiglossy, tan, smooth, with punctiform hilum in notch.

Notes: Herbaceous annual of the Mediterranean region, occasionally cultivated and naturalized and becoming weedy along roadsides and in fields and waste places in southeastern United States and Washington to California.

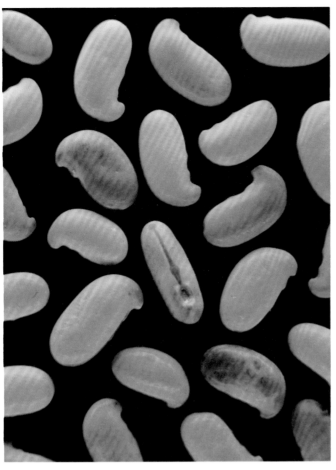

Maackia amurensis 3.2X

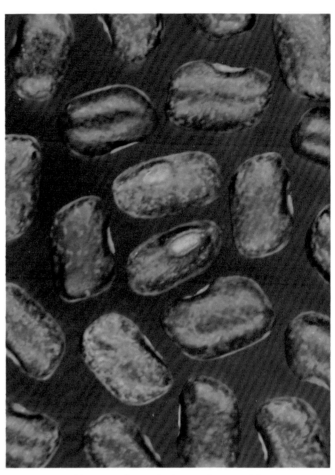

Macroptilium lathyroides 9.6X

Marina parryi 7.2X

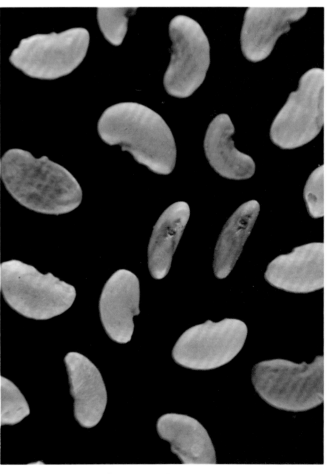

Medicago arabica 9.6X

77

Medicago Linnaeus
Trifolieae, Faboideae

Species: *lupulina* Linnaeus.

Common Names: Black medick, nonesuch, black-clover, hop medick.

Seed 1.6-1.8 x 1.1-1.3 x 1mm, D-shaped, compressed, semiglossy, greenish yellow to reddish brown, smooth, with punctiform hilum in notch, one-seeded indehiscent fruit 2-2.5 x 1.5-2 x 1.5 mm, D-shaped, compressed, dull, black, ribbed, usually with small calyx.

Notes: Herbaceous annual to perennial of Eurasia, occasionally cultivated and naturalized in waste places, roadsides, pastures, gardens, and lawns as a weed in United States and southern Canada.

Medicago Linnaeus
Trifolieae, Faboideae

Species: *orbicularis* (Linnaeus) Bartalini.

Common Names: Buttonclover.

Seed 2.5-3 x 2-3 x 1.5 mm, roughly triangular, compressed, dull, reddish tan to tan, tuberculate, with punctiform hilum in notch and concealed by whitish funicular remnant.

Notes: Herbaceous annual of Europe, naturalized and cultivated for pasture and hay in high-lime soils of Texas and California.

Medicago Linnaeus
Trifolieae, Faboideae

Species: *polymorpha* Linnaeus.

Common Name: California burclover.

Seed 2.3-4 x 1.2-2.3 x 0.8-1.5 mm, C-shaped or nearly so, compressed, semiglossy, tan to reddish brown, smooth, with punctiform hilum in notch and often partially concealed by whitish funicular remnant.

Notes: Herbaceous annual of Eurasia, naturalized along roadsides, in fields, waste places, and lawns (where weedy) throughout most of the United States, especially southern and western. Cultivated in range pastures and as a cover or green manure crop in the coastal area from Washington to California, in the Arizona foothills, and eastern Texas. California burclover usually is referred to as *Medicago hispida* Gaertner in U.S. floras.

Medicago Linnaeus
Trifolieae, Faboideae

Species: *sativa* Linnaeus.

Common Names: Alfalfa, lucerne or luzerne.

Seed 2.3-2.6 x 1.3-1.5 x 1 mm, C-shaped to angular at one or both ends, compressed, dull, yellow to green or brown (rarely white or black), smooth, with punctiform hilum in notch.

Notes: Herbaceous perennial of Eurasia, a major forage crop (12.15 million hectares planted in United States) and naturalized especially along roadsides and railroad tracks throughout the United States and Canada. Frequently referred to as "queen of the forage crops." *Medicago sativa* is a species complex composed of ten subspecies, and three are commonly found in United States: subsp. *falcata* (Linnaeus) Arcangeli, subsp. *sativa,* and subsp. x *varia* (Martyn) Arcangeli which is a hybrid between the first two (Gunn, Skrdla, and Spencer, 1978).

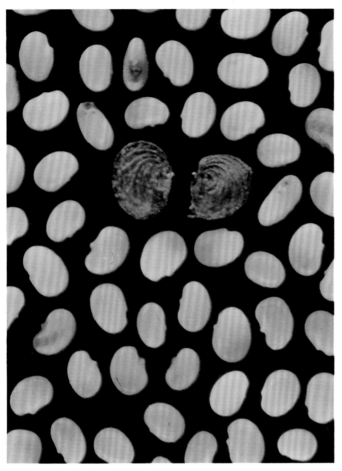

Medicago lupulina 8.0X

Medicago orbicularis 9.6X

Medicago polymorpha 9.6X

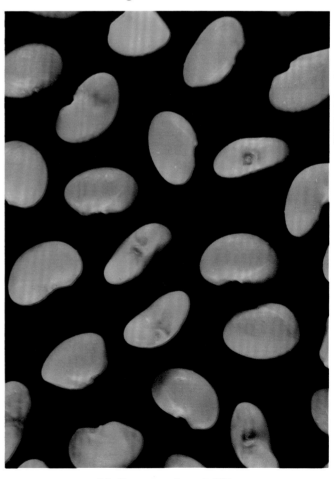

Medicago sativa 9.6X

Melilotus Miller
Trifolieae, Faboideae

Species: *alba* Medikus.

Common Names: White sweetclover, white melilot.

Seed 1.8-2.5 x 1.5-1.7 x 1 mm, mitten shaped, compressed, dull, reddish tan to reddish brown, smooth, with punctiform hilum in notch and concealed by whitish funicular remnant. One-seeded indehiscent fruit 3-4 x 1.5-2 x 1.5 mm, elliptic, compressed or nearly so, dull, tan, reticulate, with or without calyx covering less than one-half of fruit.

Notes: Herbaceous annual to biennial of Eurasia, naturalized along roadsides and in fields and waste places (becoming weedy) throughout the United States and Canada. White sweetclover is a source of nectar for honey production and occasionally is grown as a forage or green manure crop.

Melilotus Miller
Trifolieae, Faboideae

Species: *indica* (Linnaeus) Allioni.

Common Names: Sourclover, annual yellow sweetclover, bitterclover.

Seed 1.7-2 x 1.3-1.5 x 1 mm, mitten shaped, compressed, dull, tan to reddish brown, tuberculate, with punctiform hilum in notch and partially concealed by whitish funicular ring. One-seeded indehiscent fruit 2.5-3 x 1.7-2.1 x 1.5 mm, elliptic, compressed, dull, tan, reticulate, usually with calyx covering nearly one-half of fruit.

Notes: Herbaceous annual of Eurasia, naturalized in waste places (becoming weedy) throughout most of the United States. Sourclover is a green manure crop of California and coastal southeastern United States.

Melilotus Miller
Trifolieae, Faboideae

Species: *officinalis* Lamarck.

Common Name: Yellow sweetclover.

Seed 1.7-2.1 x 1.2-1.5 x 1 mm, mitten shaped, compressed, semiglossy, tan and with or without purple mottling, smooth, with punctiform hilum in notch and with or without whitish funicular ring. One-seeded indehiscent fruit 2.5-3 x 1.7-2 x 1.5 mm, elliptic, compressed, dull, dark brown, reticulate, usually with calyx covering nearly one-half of fruit.

Notes: Herbaceous biennial of Eurasia, naturalized in fields and waste places and along roadsides throughout northern United States. Yellow sweetclover is cultivated for hay, pasture, and green manure and is more tolerant of drought and competition, and is finer stemmed but lower yielding than *Melilotus alba*.

Mimosa Linnaeus
Mimoseae, Mimosoideae

Species: *borealis* A. Gray.

Common Name: Mimosa.

Seed 5-7.5 x 3.8-5.2 x 2-4 mm, circular to oblong, compressed to subterete, semiglossy, dark reddish brown, with 90% pleurogram on each face with irregularly shaped areole, with punctiform subapical hilum.

Notes: Prickly erect shrub of roadsides and disturbed areas from Kansas to Colorado, south to Texas and New Mexico.

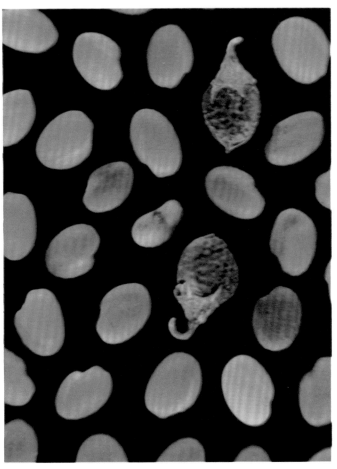

Melilotus alba 9.6X

Melilotus indica 9.6X

Melilotus officinalis 9.6X

Mimosa borealis 4.8X

81

Mimosa Linnaeus
Mimoseae, Mimosoideae

Species: *dysocarpa* Bentham.

Common Name: Mimosa

Seed 3.5-5.5 x 2.8-3.8 x 1-2 mm, ovate to irregular, compressed, glossy, dark reddish brown, with 90% pleurogram on each face and occasionally some seeds pitted, with punctiform subapical hilum. Loment 4.8-6 x 4-4.8 x 2-4 mm, square, compressed to subterete, dull, reddish tan, densely covered with tan hairs.

Notes: Spiny sprawling shrub of grasslands, rocky hillsides, and canyons of Texas and Arizona. Two varieties are recognized in the United States: Var. *dysocarpa* and var. *wrightii* (A. Gray) Kearney and Peebles.

Mimosa Linnaeus
Mimoseae, Mimosoideae

Species: *pigra* Linnaeus var. *berlandieri* (A. Gray) B. L. Turner.

Common Name: Texas mimosa.

Seed 5.7-7 x 2.4-2.5 x 2 mm, oblong, compressed, semiglossy, brown, with 90% pleurogram on each face and with or without parallel fracture lines, with punctiform subapical hilum.

Notes: Prickly erect shrub of borders of wet or low areas of Texas. Variety *pigra* of tropical America does not occur in the United States (Isley, 1981).

Mimozyganthus Burkart
Mimozygantheae, Mimosoideae

Species: *carinatus* (Grisebach) Burkart.

Common Name: Mimozyganthus.

Seed 5.2-7.3 x 5.4-7.5 x 1-1.8 mm, ovate to circular or subtrapeziform, flattened, glossy, medium to dark brown or brownish-gray, rugose, with punctiform subapical hilum. One-seeded indehiscent fruit 20-35 x 8-15 x 1-2 mm, elliptic to obovate, flattened, dull, ochre to tan, reticulate.

Notes: Spiny shrub to tree which is not present in United States. Selected to represent the monotypic tribe Mimozygantheae of tropical America.

Mucuna Adanson
Erythrininae, Phaseoleae, Faboideae

Species: *deeringiana* (Bortero) Merrill.

Common Name: Velvetbean.

Seed 11-14 x 10-12 x 8-9 mm, oblong to circular, compressed to subterete, semiglossy, ivory mottled and streaked with reddish brown, smooth, with oblong marginal hilum with tongue aril and surrounded by tan collar.

Notes: Herbaceous annual vine of southern Asia, naturalized in old fields of south Florida and cultivated in Georgia and Florida as a pasture crop. Previously known as *Stizolobium deeringianum* Bort.

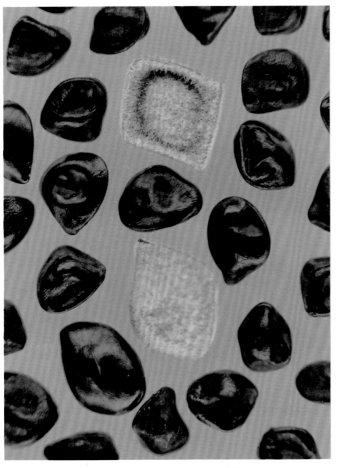

Mimosa dysocarpa 6.4X

Mimosa pigra var. *berlandieri* 4.8X

Mimozyganthus carinatus 4.8X

Mucuna deeringiana 3.2X

Mucuna Adanson
Erythrininae, Phaseoleae, Faboideae

Species: *pruriens* (Linnaeus) de Candolle.

Common Name: Cowage velvetbean.

Seed 13-18 x 9-12 x 7-8 mm, oblong, compressed, glossy, black or ivory to ivory mottled with black, smooth, with oblong marginal hilum with tongue-aril and surrounded by whitish collar.

Notes: Perennial vine of tropical Asia, cultivated and naturalized in margins of pinelands of southern Florida. Plants are covered with stinging hairs.

Mucuna Adanson
Erythrininae, Phaseoleae, Faboideae

Species: *sloanei* Fawcett & Rendle.

Common Name: Seabean.

Seed 23-33 x 23-33 x 16-20 mm, circular or nearly so, compressed, semiglossy to dull, dark reddish brown to brown, minutely tuberculate, with linear black hilum occupying three-quarters of seed circumference and surrounded by tan eye.

Notes: Perennial vine of hammocks of southern Florida. Plants are covered with stinging hairs. Seeds drift to Atlantic and Gulf beaches from tropical America.

Neptunia Loureiro
Mimoseae, Mimosoideae

Species: *pubescens* Bentham.

Common Name: Yellow puff.

Seed 4-4.5 x 2.7-3 x 1 mm, oblong, compressed, glossy, brown, with 90% pleurogram on each face and with or without parallel fracture lines, with punctiform subapical hilum.

Notes: Herbaceous prostrate perennial of southern coastal plain from Florida to Texas. Two varieties are recognized: Var. *pubescens* of Florida to Texas and var. *microcarpa* (Rose) Windler of southern Texas.

Nissolia Jacquin
Aeschynomeneae, Faboideae

Species: *schottii* (Torrey) A. Gray.

Common Name: Nissolia.

Seed 3.5-4 x 2.2-2.5 x 1-2 mm, somewhat falcate, compressed, semiglossy, reddish brown, covered with hairlike endocarp tissue, with punctiform hilum in notch.

Notes: Herbaceous perennial vine of the mountains of Pima County, Arizona.

Mucana pruriens 2.8X

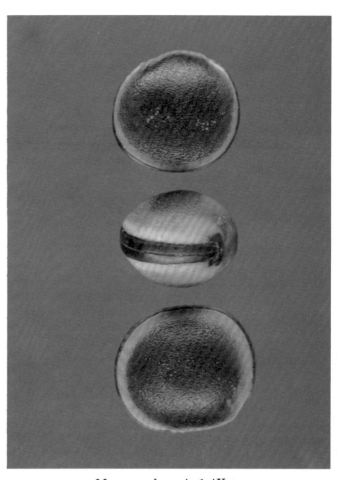

Mucuna sloanei 1.4X

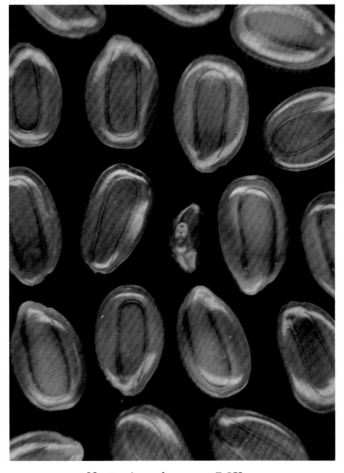

Neptunia pubescens 7.2X

Nissolia schottii 4.8X

Olneya A. Gray
Robineae, Faboideae

Species: *tesota* A. Gray.

Common Name: Desert-ironwood, Arizona-ironwood, tesota, palo de hierra.

Seed 9-10 x 6.5-7.5 x 6-7 mm, oblong to subcircular, compressed to terete, semiglossy, dark reddish brown to blackish, with scattered pits and oblong marginal hilum concealed by whitish funicular remnant.

Notes: Tree or creosote bush scrub from Colorado to New Mexico and California. Occasionally planted in treeless arid areas.

Onobrychis Miller
Hedysareae, Faboideae

Species: *viciifolia* Scopoli.

Common Name: Sainfoin.

Seed 4.3-4.8 x 2.5-3 x 2 mm, C-shaped, compressed, semiglossy, brown, smooth, with circular marginal hilum bearing rim-aril. One-seeded indehiscent fruit 7-9 x 4.5-6 x 4 mm, D-shaped, compressed, dull, tan, strongly reticulate ribbed with some ribs ending in spines and interstices bearing gray hairs with spiny crest or curved margin.

Notes: Herbaceous perennial of Mediterranean region, occasionally cultivated where alfalfa will not do well and naturalized throughout northern United States. In U.S. floras the species name is spelled *viciaefolia*.

Ononis Linnaeus
Trifolieae, Faboideae

Species: *spinosa* Linnaeus.

Common Name: Restharrow.

Seed 2.3-2.7 x 1.6-2.1 x 1.5-2 mm, mitten shaped, compressed to subterete, dull, greenish tan to reddish brown, tuberculate, with punctiform hilum in notch and subtended by brown raphe.

Notes: Herbaceous perennial of Europe, adventive in waste places of eastern United States.

Ophrestia H. M. L. Forbes
Ophrestiinae, Phaseoleae, Faboideae

Species: *radicosa* (A. Richards) Verdcourt.

Common Name: Ophrestia.

Seed 4-5 x 3-3.5 x 2 mm, oblong, compressed, glossy, reddish to greenish brown, smooth, with oblong marginal hilum concealed by honey colored aril and bearing tongue-aril.

Notes: Herbaceous perennial which is not in United States. Ophrestia was selected to represent the subtribe Ophrestiinae composed of three genera in South Africa.

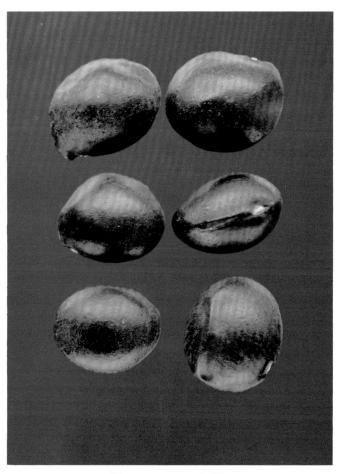

Olneya tesota 3.2X

Onobrychis viciifolia 4.0X

Ononis spinosa 9.6X

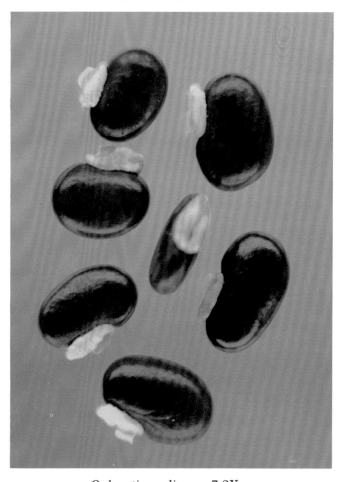

Ophrestia radicosa 7.2X

Orbexilum Rafinesque
Psoraleeae, Faboideae

Species: *pedunculatum* Rydberg.

Common Name: Sampson's snakeroot.

Seed 2.8-3.2 x 2.4-2.6 x 2 mm, D-shaped, compressed, glossy, dark reddish brown, smooth, with circular marginal hilum concealed by funicular remnant. One-seeded indehiscent fruit 3.7-4.3 x 3.5 x 2.5 mm, subcircular, compressed, dull, tan to brown (if tan then reddish brown in area where calyx covered fruit), reticulate.

Notes: Herbaceous perennial of dry open woods, clearings and fields from Virginia to Kansas, south to Georgia and Texas. Sampson's snakeroot is referred to as *Psoralea psoraloides* (Walter) Cory in U.S. floras.

Ornithopus Linnaeus
Coronilleae, Faboideae

Species: *sativus* Brotero.

Common Name: Serradela.

Seed 1.8-2.2 x 1.2-1.7 x 1 mm, oblong, compressed, semiglossy, reddish brown, smooth, with punctiform marginal hilum bearing rim-aril and surrounded by black eye. Loment 2.8-3.2 x 2.4-2.6 x 1.7-2 mm, oblong with truncate end, compressed, dull, tan, reticulately ribbed with gray hairs in interstices.

Notes: Herbaceous annual of the Mediterranean region, naturalized in sandy soils of Long Island, New York.

Oxytropis de Candolle
Galegeae Faboideae

Species: *campestris* (Linnaeus) de Candolle.

Common Name: Crazyweed.

Seed 1.5-2 x 1.5-1.9 x 1 mm, mitten shaped, compressed, dull, reddish brown mottled and streaked or not by black, smooth, with circular hilum in notch concealed by whitish funicular remnant or partially concealed by whitish rim-aril.

Notes: Herbaceous perennial of sandy plains and bench lands from North Dakota to Montana, south to Colorado and Utah.

Oxytropis de Candolle
Galegeae, Faboideae

Species: *sericea* Nuttall.

Common Name: White locoweed, crazyweed.

Seed 1.7-2.2 x 1.5-2 x 1-1.2 mm, mitten shaped, compressed, dull, reddish brown, smooth, with punctiform hilum in notch and with or without whitish rim-aril.

Notes: Herbaceous perennial of the plains from South Dakota to Montana, south to Texas and New Mexico.

Orbexilum pedunculatum 4.8X

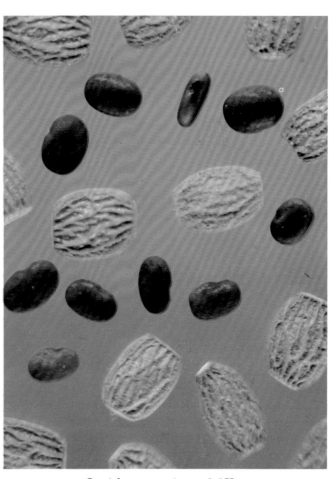

Ornithopus sativus 8.0X

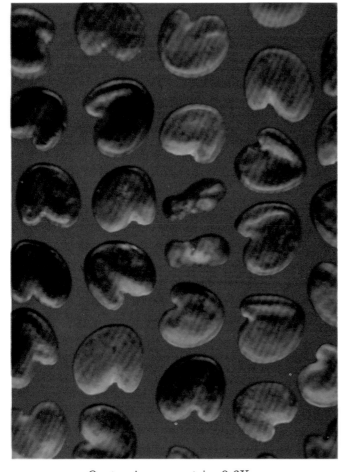

Oxytropis campestris 9.6X

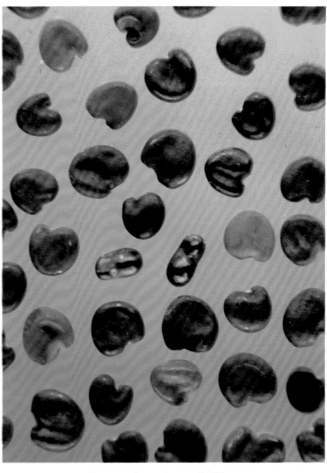

Oxytropis sericea 8.0X

89

Pachyrrhizus A. Richard ex de Candolle
Diocleinae, Phaseoleae, Faboideae

Species: *erosus* (Linnaeus) Urban.

Common Name: Yam-bean.

Seed 7-9 x 7-7.5 x 5-6 mm, oblong to subcircular, compressed, semiglossy, reddish brown, smooth, with elliptic marginal hilum bearing tongue-aril.

Notes: Herbaceous perennial twining to erect of New World tropics, cultivated for edible roots and naturalized in southern Florida. Seeds of yam-bean are poisonous.

Parkia R. Brown
Parkieae, Mimosoideae

Species: *javanica* Merrill.

Common Name: Parkia.

Seed 15-17 x 8-12 x 6-7 mm, oblong to subcircular, compressed, semiglossy, blackish brown, with 100% pleurogram on each face and punctiform apical hilum.

Notes: Tree which is not present in the United States. Selected to represent the two-genus tribe Parkieae of the tropics.

Parkinsonia Linnaeus
Caesalpinieae, Caesalpinioideae

Species: *aculeata* Linnaeus.

Common Name: Jerusalem-thorn, retama, horse-bean, Mexican palo verde.

Seed 9-9.5 x 3.3-4.2 x 2-4 mm, oblong, compressed to terete, glossy, yellowish brown mottled and streaked with brown, usually with blackish raphe and concentric fracture lines, with punctiform subapical hilum.

Notes: Tree in variety of habitats from South Carolina to California and widely cultivated within its range.

Parryella Torrey & Gray ex A. Gray
Amorpheae, Faboideae

Species: *filifolia* Torrey & Gray.

Common Name: Dunebroom.

Seed 3.5-4.5 x 2-2.4 x 2 mm, elliptic with notch to falcate, compressed to terete, semiglossy, tan to reddish brown, smooth, with circular hilum in notch surrounded by dark collar and subtended by darker raphe. One-seeded indehiscent fruit 7-8 x 2.5-3 x 2-3 mm, fusiform, terete, dull, tan, dotted with large amber glands, with persistent style and calyx.

Notes: Shrub of treeless sandy plains from Utah to New Mexico and Arizona.

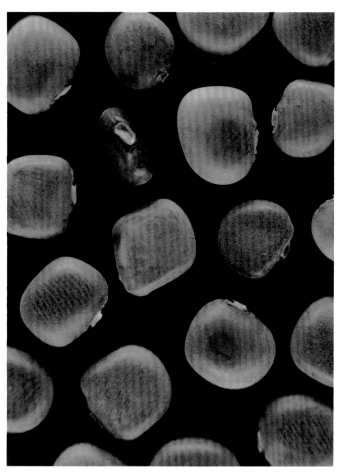

Pachyrrhizus erosus 3.2X

Parkia javanica 3.2X

Parkinsonia aculeata 4.0X

Parryella filifolia 7.2X

Peltophorum (Vogel) Bentham
Caesalpinieae, Caesalpinioideae

Species: *pterocarpum* (A. P. de Candolle) Backer ex K. Heyne.

Common Names: Yellow-poinciana, yellow flamboyant.

Seed 10-11 x 4.5-5 x 2 mm, oblong, flattened, glossy, tannish brown, with reticulate fracture lines, with punctiform subapicial hilum concealed by brown funicular remnant.

Notes: Tree of tropical Asia, commonly cultivated in the Miami area and adventive in Florida. Previously known as *Peltophorum inerme* Roxburgh.

Peteria A. Gray
Robineae, Faboideae

Species: *thompsonae* S. Watson.

Common Name: Peteria.

Seed 5.3-5.8 x 3.8 x 2.7 mm, oblong, compressed, semiglossy, tan mottled with purple, smooth, with oblong marginal hilum bearing minute tongue-aril.

Notes: Herbaceous perennial of the desert shrub community of Utah to northern Arizona.

Phaseolus Linnaeus
Phaseolinae, Phaseoleae, Faboideae

Species: *coccineus* Linnaeus.

Common Name: Scarlet runner bean or runner bean.

Seed 12-22 x 10-14 x 6-8 mm, oblong to somewhat C-shaped, compressed, semiglossy, reddish brown to ivory and with or without blackish to reddish brown mottling which may coalesce, smooth, with oblong marginal hilum concealed by white funicular remnant and for ivory mottled seeds surrounded with dark eye.

Notes: Herbaceous perennial (treated as an annual in the United States) of Mexico, cultivated as an ornamental vine with edible seeds. Seed sold in flower and vegetable seed packet trade.

Phaseolus Linnaeus
Phaseolinae, Phaseoleae, Faboideae

Species: *lunatus* Linnaeus.

Common Name: Lima bean.

Seed 9-25 x 7-16 x 3-6 mm, oblong, compressed, semiglossy to dull, variously colored (ivory, dark to light reddish brown, blackish brown) and with or without darker colored mottles which may coalesce into solid colors causing seed to be bicolored, with inconspicuous to conspicuous fanlike striations on each face, with oblong marginal hilum concealed by whitish funicular remnant.

Notes: Herbaceous annual of Mexico, widely cultivated throughout the United States for its edible seeds. Many cultivars are available in the vegetable seed packet and commercial trade.

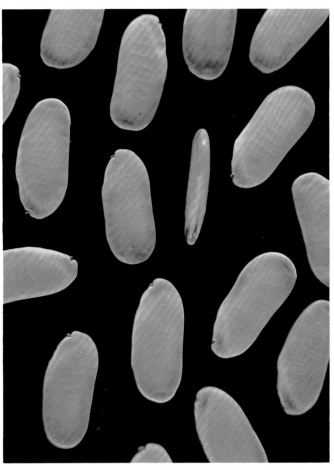

Peltophorum pterocarpum 3.2X

Peteria thompsonae 8.8X

Phaseolus coccineus 2.2X

Phaseolus lunatus 1.8X

Phaseolus Linnaeus
Phaseolinae, Phaseoleae, Faboideae

Species: *vulgaris* Linnaeus.

Common Name: Garden bean, bush bean, pole bean, field bean.

Seed 6.5-20 x 4.5-10 x 3-7 mm, oblong to C-shaped, compressed to terete, glossy, variously colored (white, dark to light reddish brown, tan, black, with or without darker mottling which may be separate or coalesced forming bicolored seeds), smooth, with oblong marginal hilum concealed by whitish funicular remnant.

Notes: Herbaceous annual either erect or vining of Mexico, widely cultivated for its edible seeds throughout the United States. Many cultivars are available in the vegetable seed packet and commercial trade. Humans should not eat raw seeds or raw green pods.

Pickeringia Nuttall ex Torrey & Gray
Thermopsideae, Faboideae

Species: *montana* Nuttall ex Torrey & Gray var. *tomentosa* (Abrams) I. M. Johnston.

Common Name: Chaparral-pea.

Seed 3.7-4.3 x 2.2-2.5 xs 1.5 mm, oblong, compressed, dull, black, smooth, with punctiform marginal hilum.

Notes: Spiny shrub on dry slopes and ridges, chaparral, and mixed evergreen stands of cismontane California. Two varieties are recognized in United States: Var. *montana* and var. *tomentosa* (Abrams) I. M. Johnston. Variety *montana* rarely sets fruits; it spreads by underground stems especially after fires, while var. *tomentosa* of the San Diego area fruits abundantly.

Piscidia Linnaeus
Millettieae, Faboideae

Species: *piscipula* (Linnaeus) Sargent.

Common Name: Jamaica-dogwood.

Seed 6-8 x 3.2-4 x 2.5-3 mm, oblong, compressed, semiglossy, reddish brown to black, smooth, with oblong marginal hilum within tan collar and surrounded by poorly defined darker colored eye.

Notes: Tree of the coastal strand of southern Florida.

Pisum Linnaeus
Vicieae, Faboideae

Species: *sativum* Linnaeus.

Common Name: Garden pea, English pea, field pea.

Seed 5-11 x 5-9 x 5-8 mm, circular or nearly so, terete or nearly so, dull, either ochre (with or without greenish cast) or dark to light reddish brown and lighter colored mottled or not with darker reddish brown, smooth to rugose, with elliptic marginal hilum either color of seed or much darker than seed.

Notes: Herbaceous annual vine to erect of Eurasia, widely cultivated throughout the United States for home gardens, in Great Lake and Pacific northwest states for processing, and Pacific northwest for mature seed. Included in this seed description and illustration are edible pea, field pea (formerly known as variety, subspecies, or species *arvense* (Linnaeus) Poiret, and subspecies or species *elatius* M. Biebestein).

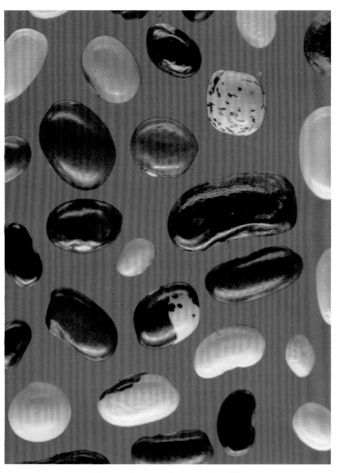

Phaseolus vulgaris 2.4X

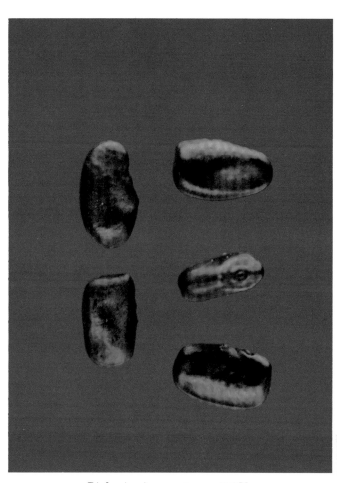

Pickeringia montana 7.2X

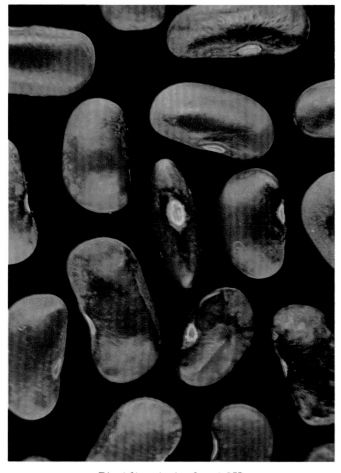

Piscidia piscipula 4.8X

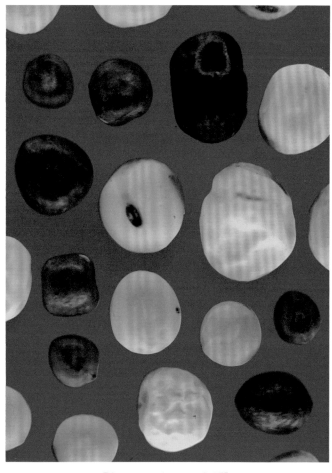

Pisum sativum 3.2X

Pithecellobium Martius
Ingeae, Mimosoideae

Species: *dulce* (Roxburgh) Bentham.

Common Name: Tamarind.

Seed 9-10 x 7-8 x 3-4 mm, irregular, compressed, semiglossy, dark reddish brown (almost black) with 90% pleurogram on each face, with punctiform apical hilum concealed or not by reddish brown funicular remnant.

Notes: Annual to unarmed shrub or small tree of Old World, cultivated and adventive in southern Florida and Texas.

Podalyria Willdenow
Podalyrieae, Faboideae

Species: *calyptrata* (Retzius) Willdenow.

Common Name: Podalyria.

Seed 4.5-6 x 3.5-4.5 x 2 mm, oblong, compressed, glossy, tan to reddish brown without or with one to two darker reddish brown mottles, smooth, with oblong marginal hilum concealed by ivory rim-aril and surrounded by slightly darker collar and subtended by darker raphe.

Notes: Shrub not present in the United States. Selected to represent the three-genus tribe Podalyrieae of the Cape region of South Africa

Pongamia Ventenat
Millettieae, Faboideae

Species: *pinnata* (Linnaeus) Merrill.

Common Name: Pongam.

Seed 18-20 x 15-16 x 4-5 mm, circular to oblong, compressed, dull, reddish brown, rugose, with punctiform marginal hilum concealed by reddish brown funicular remnant. One-seeded indehiscent fruit 42-45 x 23-25 x 12-13 mm, oblong, compressed, dull, dirty brown, somewhat rugose.

Notes: Tree of Ceylon, cultivated in southern Florida.

Prosopis Linnaeus
Mimoseae, Mimosoideae

Species: *glandulosa* Torrey.

Common Name: Mesquite.

Seed 6.3-7 x 4.4-4.6 x 2-3 mm, oblong, compressed, semiglossy, brown, with 90% pleurogram on each face and reticulate fracture lines, with punctiform apical hilum. Article (endocarp of indehiscent fruit) 9-13 x 7-8 x 3-4 mm, more or less elliptic or rhombic, compressed, dull, reddish tan, with honey-combed surface to faintly rugose.

Notes: Small tree to large shrub of lower mountain slopes, mesas, and desert grassland ranges of southcentral and southwestern states. Mesquite is a serious weed. Two varieties are recognized in United States: Var. *glandulosa* and var. *torreyana* (L. Benson) I. M. Johnston. It also is known in U.S. floras as *Prosopis juliflora* auct.

Pithecellobium dulce 3.2X

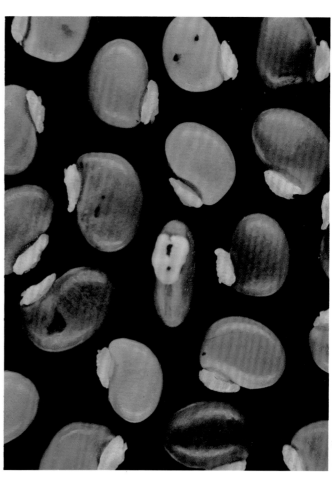

Podalyria calyptrata 4.8X

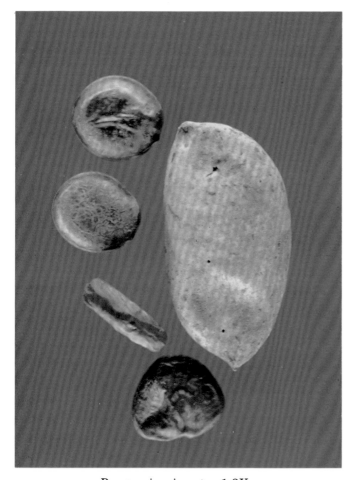

Pongamia pinnata 1.3X

Prosopis glandulosa 3.2X

97

Psoralea Linnaeus
Psoraleeae, Faboideae

Species: *bituminosa* Linnaeus.

Common Name: Psoralea.

Seed coat adnate to fruit. One-seeded indehiscent fruit 12-15 x 3-3.5 x 1-2 mm, oblong with prominent beak, compressed, dull, brown with tan beak, with diverse ornamentation (silvery to dark brown hairs, black to brown spines, and rudimentary black to brown spines), without or with calyx with 5 prominent teeth.

Notes: Semishrub of Old World, naturalized and cultivated in California. Seeds do not occur outside the fruits. Only the embryo can be separated from the indehiscent fruit.

Psoralea Linnaeus
Psoraleeae, Faboideae

Species: *orbicularis* Lindley.

Common Name: Psoralea.

Seed 4-5 x 2.8-3.2 x 2 mm, oblong, compressed, semiglossy, reddish brown to brown mottled (often faintly) with black, smooth, with elliptic marginal hilum with rim-aril and surrounded by lighter colored collar. One-seeded indehiscent fruit 6-7.5 x 3.5-4 x 2 mm, D-shaped, compressed, dull, brown, reticulate and bearing whitish hairs.

Notes: Herbaceous perennial of moist places of California.

Psorothamnus Rydberg
Amorpheae, Faboideae

Species: *arborescens* (Torrey) Barneby var. *minutifolius* (Parish) Barneby.

Common Name: Smoke shrub.

Seed 4.5-5.3 x 3.5-4 x 2-3 mm, barely falcate, compressed, glossy, reddish brown to reddish tan, mottled or not with minute purple dots, rugose, with circular hilum in notch with whitish rim-aril. One-seeded indehiscent fruit 9-10 x 4.3-6 x 3 mm, D-shaped, compressed, semiglossy, reddish brown, rugose and glandularly dotted.

Notes: Shrub with or without thorns of rocky sandy desert hillsides from Nevada to California.

Psorothamnus Rydberg
Amorpheae, Faboideae

Species: *scoparius* (A. Gray) Rydberg.

Common Name: Psorothamnus.

Seed 2-2.5 x 1.5-1.7 x 1 mm, oblong, compressed, glossy, greenish tan to tan mottled with reddish brown, smooth, with circular marginal hilum surrounded by collar. One-seeded indehiscent fruit, nearly concealed by calyx bearing short white hairs and light reddish brown glands, 4.5-5 x 2.5 x 2 mm, oblong, compressed, dull, tan, surface nearly concealed by short white hairs and light reddish brown glands.

Notes: Shrub to subshrub of dunes and sandy river beds from Texas to New Mexico.

Psoralea bituminosa 3.2X

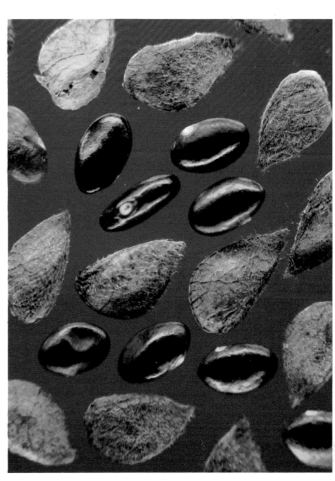

Psoralea orbicularis 4.8X

Psorothamnus arborescens var. *minutifolia* 4.8X

Psorothamnus scoparius 9.6X

Pueraria de Candolle
Glycininae, Phaseoleae, Faboideae

Species: *lobata* (Willdenow) Ohwi.

Common Names: Kudzu or kudzu vine.

Seed 2.8-4 x 2-2.7 x 2 mm, oblong, compressed or nearly so, glossy, reddish brown mottled with black, smooth, with oblong marginal hilum with rim-aril.

Notes: Herbaceous perennial of China, naturalized along roadsides and rivers throughout southeastern United States, usually south of the Ohio River valley. Kudzu seldom flowers north of Virginia. Originally introduced into United States for its edible starchy roots used for human food, it was found to produce good hay and forage, and to be valuable for erosion control. Kudzu is now a serious weed because it smothers native vegetation. Previously known as *Pueraria thunbergiana* Bentham.

Rhynchosia Loureiro
Cajaninae, Phaseoleae, Faboideae

Species: *minima* (Linnaeus) de Candolle.

Common Name: Small-leaved snoutbean.

Seed 2.9-3.5 x 2.5-2.8 x 2 mm, oblong, compressed, semiglossy, ivory to brown mottled with dark brown to black, smooth, with oblong marginal hilum concealed by grayish funicular remnant and surrounded by reddish brown collar.

Notes: Herbaceous perennial vine of Old World, naturalized in coastal areas of South Carolina, Florida, and Texas. Two varieties are recognized in the United States: Var. *minima* and var. *diminifolia* Walraven.

Robinia Linnaeus
Robineae, Faboideae

Species: *pseudoacacia* Linnaeus.

Common Names: Black locust, false-acacia, yellow locust.

Seed 3.2-4.2 x 2.7-3 x 2 mm, somewhat falcate, compressed, glossy, reddish brown mottled dark reddish brown, smooth, with circular hilum in notch with or without tongue-aril.

Notes: Tree of roadsides from Pennsylvania to Indiana and Oklahoma, south to Georgia and Louisiana, and escaped throughout most of the United States. Black locust is planted as a shade tree and for its durable wood. The seeds and bark are somewhat poisonous. In some U.S. floras the species name is spelled *pseudo-acacia*.

Schrankia Willdenow
Mimoseae, Mimosoideae

Species: *uncinata* Willdenow.

Common Name: Sensitive brier.

Seed 3-4.5 x 2-3.2 x 2 mm, oblong-angular, compressed to terete, glossy, reddish brown to brown with golden patches caused by raised cuticle, with 90% pleurogram and usually two longitudinal grooves on each face, with punctiform apical hilum.

Notes: Prickly herbaceous perennial of sandy woodlands and waste places in Georgia and Florida.

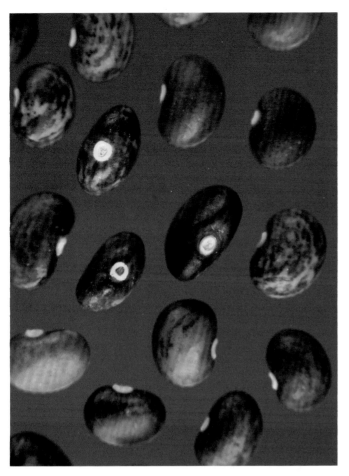

Pueraria lobata 7.2X

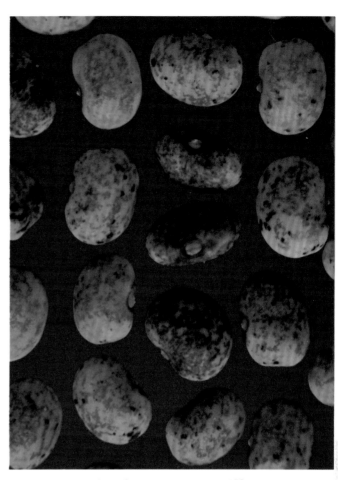

Rhynchosia minima 7.2X

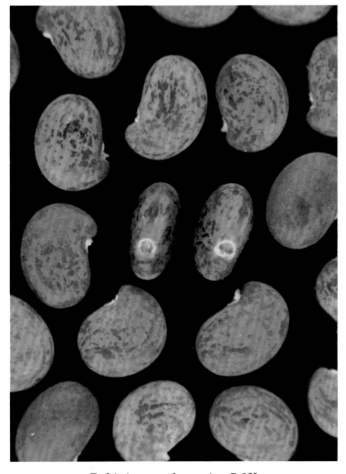

Robinia pseudoacacia 7.2X

Schrankia uncinata 7.2X

Scorpiurus Linnaeus
Coronilleae, Faboideae

Species: *muricatus* Linnaeus.

Common Name: Scorpiurus.

Seed 2.7-4.2 x 1.7-2 x 2 mm, C-shaped, terete, dull, reddish brown to tan, faintly rugose, with circular marginal hilum concealed by whitish funicular remnant and surrounded by blackish eye. Loment 3-6 x 1.7-2 x 2-3 mm, arcuate to nearly circular, terete, dull, tan, with ribs which may be tuberculate to spiny.

Notes: Herbaceous annual of southern Europe, waif in northern United States. Referred to in U. S. floras as either *Scorpiurus sulcatus* Linnaeus or *Scorpiurus subvillosus* Linnaeus.

Senna Miller
Cassieae, Caesalpinioideae

Species: *alata* (Linnaeus) Roxburgh.

Common Names: Candlesticks, candle tree.

Seed 5.2-6.5 x 4.5-5.5 x 1.5-2 mm, rhomboid, compressed, semiglossy, reddish and greenish and blackish brown, with 100% pseudopleurogram enclosing a greenish to blackish areole bearing parallel fracture lines and pitted over rest of surface and bearing longitudinal rib on each face, with punctiform subapical hilum.

Notes: Tree of South America, cultivated along Gulf Coast and in southern California and naturalized in Florida. Seeds of *Senna alata* are unusual in the family because they are compressed at an oblique angle to the cotyledonary plane. The longitudinal facial ribs are edges of the cotyledons. Previously known as *Cassia alata* Linnaeus.

Senna Miller
Cassieae, Caesalpinioideae

Species: *didymobotrya* (Fresenius) Irwin & Barneby.

Common Name: Senna.

Seed 9-10 x 4.7-5 x 2-3 mm, oblong with prominent radicle lobe, compressed, semiglossy, brown, with 100% pseudopleurogram enclosing a glossy brown areole bearing reticulate fracture lines and on outside of pseudopleurogram on each face and reticulate fracture lines in cuticle (if cuticle exfoliated, fracture lines absent), with punctiform subapical hilum.

Notes: Shrub of Africa, naturalized along roadsides in Florida and cultivated in California. Previously known as *Cassia didymobotrya* Fresenius.

Senna Miller
Cassieae, Caesalpinioideae

Species: *occidentalis* (Linnaeus) Irwin & Barneby.

Common Names: Coffeeweed, coffee-senna, stypticweed.

Seed 4-4.5 x 2.7-4 x 2 mm, subcircular, compressed, glossy, grayish brown, with 100% pseudopleurogram on each face enclosing grayish brown areole bearing reticulate fracture lines and on outside of pseudopleurogram minutely tuberculate, with punctiform subapical hilum.

Notes: Herbaceous annual of the tropics, naturalized and becoming weedy along roadsides and in waste places more or less south of 36 degree latitude. Although coffeeweed seeds have been used as a coffee substitute, the plants are poisonous to cattle. Previously known as *Cassia occidentalis* Linnaeus.

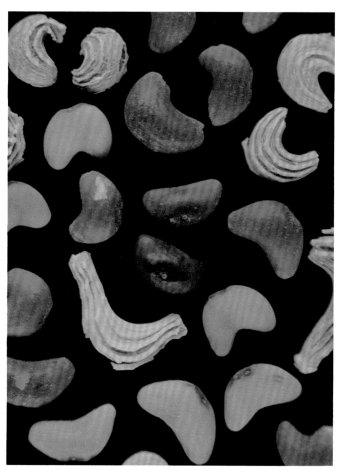

Scorpiurus muricatus 6.4X

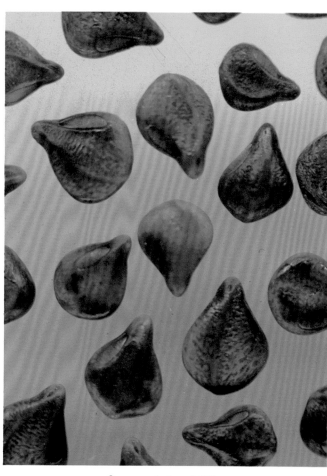

Senna alata 4.8X

Senna didymobotrya 4.8X

Senna occidentalis 6.4X

Sesbania Scopoli
Robineae, Faboideae

Species: *macrocarpa* Muhlenberg ex Rafinesque.

Common Names: Sesbania, Colorado River-hemp, wild-hemp, large indigoweed, tall-indigo, Indian-hemp.

Seed 4.3-5 x 2.3-2.7 x 2 mm, oblong, compressed, glossy, tan to reddish brown with or without blackish mottles, smooth, with circular marginal hilum with rim-aril and surrounded by darker colored eye.

Notes: Herbaceous annual of alluvial soil from Missouri south to Florida and Texas, adventive along Atlantic seaboard and in California. Sesbania is a noxious weed in irrigation ditches and rice fields of Louisiana and Texas and referred to in U. S. floras as *Sesbania exaltata* (Rafinesque) Cory.

Sophora Linnaeus
Sophoreae, Faboideae

Species: *tomentosa* Linnaeus.

Common Name: Necklace pod.

Seed 6.5-8 x 6.5-7 x 5-5.5 mm, oblong, terete, glossy, reddish brown, smooth, with oblong marginal hilum partially concealed by whitish funicular remnant and surrounded by slightly darker eye.

Notes: Shrub of coastal Florida and Texas and occasionally cultivated. Two varieties are recognized in the United States: Var. *occidentalis* (Linnaeus) Isely of southeastern Texas and var. *truncata* Torrey & Gray of southern Florida.

Spartium Linnaeus
Genisteae, Faboideae

Species: *junceum* Linnaeus.

Common Name: Spanish-broom.

Seed 3-4 x 2-3.5 x 1.5 mm, square to subcircular, compressed, glossy, reddish brown to tan, smooth, with circular marginal hilum with tongue-aril and surrounded by darker colored eye.

Notes: Shrub of Mediterranean region, naturalized in scattered dry waste places of California.

Sphaerophysa de Candolle
Galegeae, Faboideae

Species: *salsula* (Pallas) de Candolle.

Common Name: Bladder-vetch.

Seed 2.3-2.7 x 2-2.4 x 1 mm, mitten shaped, compressed, semiglossy, grayish brown to reddish brown, with faint color reticulation and circular hilum in notch and concealed by yellowish funicular remnants.

Notes: Herbaceous perennial of Asia, naturalized on alkaline or irrigated soils of western United States where it is a noxious weed. In U. S. floras bladder-vetch is known as *Swainsona salsula* (Pallas) Taubert.

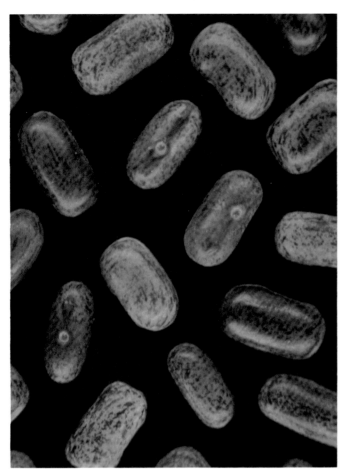

Sesbania macrocarpa 6.4X

Sophora tomentosa 3.2X

Spartium junceum 7.2X

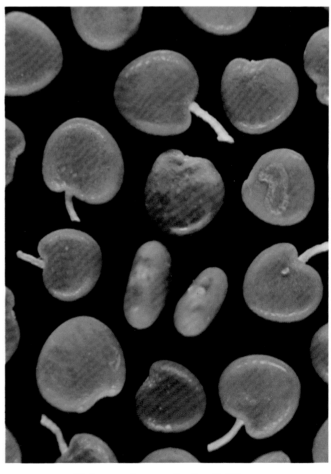

Sphaerophysa salsula 9.6X

Sphinctospermum Rose
Robinieae, Faboideae

Species: *constrictum* (S. Watson) Rose.

Common Name: Sphinctospermum.

Seed 2-2.5 x 1.6-1.8 x 1 mm, square to rectangular with constricted circumference, subterete, dull, greenish tan to reddish tan or reddish brown, tuberculate, with punctiform marginal hilum in constriction.

Notes: Herbaceous annual of sandy places of southern Arizona.

Strophostyles Elliott
Phaseolinae, Phaseoleae, Faboideae

Species: *helvola* (Linnaeus) Elliott.

Common Names: wild-bean, trailing wild-bean, peavine, beanvine, wild-bean vine.

Seed 4.5-5.7 x 3 x 2 mm, oblong, terete, dull, brown, scurfy because of adnate endocarp tissue (if removed, seed coat glossy, reddish brown mottled with black), with linear marginal hilum concealed by whitish funicular remnants and with or without tongue-aril.

Notes: Herbaceous annual vine of various habitats (beaches, open woods, open areas, old fields, etc.) from Quebec to Minnesota and South Dakota, south to Florida and Texas.

Stylosanthes Swartz
Aeschynomeneae, Faboideae

Species: *biflora* (Linnaeus) Britton, Sterns, Poggenberg.

Common Name: Pencil flower.

Seed 2-2.4 x 1.4-1.5 x 1.4-1.5 mm, subfalcate, subterete, semiglossy to dull, reddish brown, smooth, with punctiform marginal hilum surrounded by dark reddish brown eye. Loment 3-4 x 1.8-2.5 x 1.6-2 mm, D-shaped to subcircular and with or without truncate base (if without then with aborted indehiscent fruit segment that is stalk like) and apex bearing curled style, compressed to subterete, dull, greenish to reddish brown, reticulate, and bearing short white hairs.

Notes: Herbaceous perennial of dry or rocky woods from New York to Illinois and Kansas, south to Florida and Texas. Two varieties are recognized in United States: Var. *biflora* and var. *hispidissima* (Michaux) Pollard & Ball. *Stylosanthes riparia* Kearney is included in *S. biflora*.

Swartzia Schreber
Swartzieae, Faboideae

Species: *simplex* (Swartz) Sprengel.

Common Name: Swartzia.

Seed 18-23 x 9-10 x 7 mm, oblong-curved, subterete, glossy, brown, rugose, with wedge shaped marginal hilum concealed by whitish funicular remnant.

Notes: Tree not present in the United States. Selected to represent the eleven-genus tropical tribe Swartzieae.

Sphinctospermum constrictum 8.8X

Strophostyles helvola 7.2X

Stylosanthes biflora 7.2X

Swartzia simplex 3.2X

Tamarindus Linnaeus
Amherstieae, Caesalpinioideae

Species: *indica* Linnaeus.

Common Name: Tamarind.

Seed 13-18 x 9-12 x 6-10 mm, oblong to irregularly oblong, compressed to terete, areole dull and rest glossy, reddish brown, with 100% pseudopleurogram on each face enclosing areole bearing parallel and reticulate fracture lines and rest pitted and cuticle raised causing surface tod be golden dotted, with punctiform apical hilum concealed by reddish brown funicular remnant.

Notes: Tree of Africa, cultivated and perhaps naturalized in Florida. Tamarind has numerous economic uses in tropical countries.

Tephrosia Persoon
Millettieae, Faboideae

Species: *virginiana* (Linnaeus) Persoon.

Common Names: Goatsrue, catgut, rabbit-pea, devils shoestring, hoary-pea.

Seed 3.2-4.2 x 2.5-3 x 1.5 mm, oblong, compressed, semiglossy occasionally partially concealed by whitish adnate endocarp tissue, brown mottled with dark brown, smooth, with oblong marginal hilum with tongue-aril and surrounded by reddish brown eye.

Notes: Herbaceous perennial of old fields, open woods, and sandy soil from New Hampshire to Minnesota, south to Florida, Kansas and Texas.

Thermopsis R. Brown ex W. & W. T. Aiton
Thermopsideae, Faboideae

Species: *villosa* (Walter) Fernald & Schubert.

Common Name: Golden-pea.

Seed 3-4.5 x 2.8-3.2 x 2 mm, oblong, compressed, semiglossy, reddish brown mottled with black, smooth, with oblong marginal hilum with rim-aril and tongue-aril.

Notes: Herbaceous perennial of the mountains from Maryland to Georgia and Tennessee. Previously known as *Thermopsis caroliniana* M. A. Curtis.

Trifolium Linnaeus
Trifolieae, Faboideae

Species: *arvense* Linnaeus.

Common Names: Rabbitfoot clover, old-field clover, pussies, stone clover.

Seed 0.9-1.3 x 0.6-0.7 x 0.5 mm, mitten shaped, compressed, semiglossy, yellow to tan, faintly reticulate, with punctiform hilum in notch. One-seeded indehiscent fruit, concealed by hairy calyx, 1.2-1.5 x 0.7-0.8 x 0.6 mm, oblong, terete or nearly so, dull, tan, smooth.

Notes: Herbaceous annual of Europe, naturalized in waste areas on poor soils and along roadsides throughout United States.

Tamarindus indica 3.2X

Tephrosia virginiana 6.4X

Thermopsis villosa 6.4X

Trifolium arvense 9.6X

109

Trifolium Linnaeus
Trifolieae, Faboideae

Species: *dubium* Sibthorp.

Common Names: Small hop clover or little hop clover.

Seed 1.5 x 1.2 x 1 mm, mitten shaped, subterete, glossy, bicolored tan above radicle lobe and greenish tan from radicle lobe tip down, smooth, with punctiform hilum in notch. One-seeded indehiscent fruit, concealed by marcescent corolla, 2 x 1.4 x 1 mm, elliptic and tapered to stalk and style, compressed, dull, tan to brown, faintly reticulate.

Notes: Herbaceous annual of Europe, naturalized along roadsides and waste places from Nova Scotia to Indiana and Missouri, south to Alabama and Mississippi, and British Columbia to California and Texas. Small hop clover is used as a pasture plant, usually in combination with forage grasses, in the southeastern states.

Trifolium Linnaeus
Trifolieae, Faboideae

Species: *fragiferum* Linnaeus.

Common Name: Strawberry clover.

Seed 1.3-1.6 x 1-1.4 x 1-1.2 mm, mitten shaped, compressed to subterete, semiglossy, monochrome reddish brown to tan or reddish brown mottled with purple to purplish black, smooth, with punctiform hilum in notch. One-seeded indehiscent fruit, concealed by inflated calyx and marcescent corolla, 2.2-2.5 x 2.2-2.5 x 1-1.3 mm, circular, compressed, semiglossy, brown, smooth.

Notes: Herbacaeous perennial of Eurasia, naturalized in lawns of eastern United States and cultivated as a pasture legume and naturalized on the Pacific coast, especially on wet, saline soils.

Trifolium Linnaeus
Trifolieae, Faboideae

Species: *hirtum* Allioni.

Common Name: Rose clover.

Seed 1.8-2.5 x 1.5-2.2 x 1-2 mm, subcircular, terete or nearly so, semiglossy, tan, smooth, with punctiform marginal hilum. One-seeded indehiscent fruit, concealed by hairy calyx, 2-2.7 x 1.6-2.3 x 1-2 mm, subcircular, terete or nearly so, dull, brown, smooth.

Notes: Herbaceous annual of Europe, naturalized along roadsides in Virginia and North Carolina and cultivated with grasses or winter grains in southeastern states and coastal Pacific states.

Trifolium Linnaeus
Trifolieae, Faboideae

Species: *hybridum* Linnaeus.

Common Names: Alsike clover, Swedish clover.

Seed 1-1.3 x 0.9-1.3 x 0.5 mm, mitten shaped, compressed, dull, variably colored (reddish brown, tan, greenish tan mottled or not with purple or black with mottling on some seeds coalescing causing seed to be purple to blackish), smooth, with punctiform hilum in notch. One- to three-seeded indehiscent fruits, concealed by marcescent corolla, 2-4 x 1.5-2 x 1 mm, oblong, compressed, dull, greenish tan, faintly reticulate.

Notes: Herbaceous perennial of Eurasia, naturalized and cultivated in wet meadows and damp or acid places from Newfoundland to Alaska, south to Florida and California.

Trifolium dubium 9.6X

Trifolium fragiferum 8.0X

Trifolium hirtum 6.4X

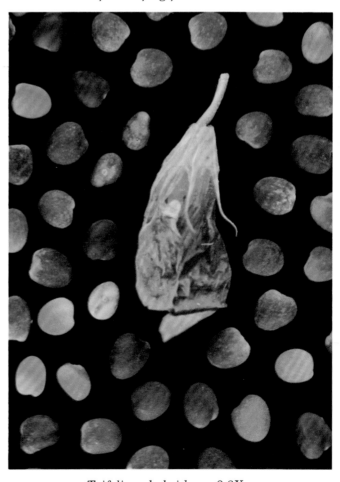

Trifolium hybridum 8.8X

111

Trifolium Linnaeus
Trifolieae, Faboideae

Species: *incarnatum* Linnaeus.

Common Name: Crimson clover.

Seed 1.9-2.3 x 1.4-1.6 x 1.5 mm, oblong, terete, glossy, buff to brown, minutely pitted, with punctiform marginal hilum. One-seeded indehiscent fruit, concealed by hairy calyx, 3.5-4 x 2 x 2 mm, oblong, terete, dull, brown, smooth.

Notes: Herbaceous annual of Europe, naturalized in waste places and fields and cultivated in southern United States, essentially south of Maryland. Crimson clover is planted with ryegrass and winter grains for pasture, hay, green chopping, or green manure.

Trifolium Linnaeus
Trifolieae, Faboideae

Species: *pratense* Linnaeus.

Common Names: Red clover, medium red clover, mammoth red clover.

Seed 1.5-2.1 x 1-1.7 x 1-1.5 mm, mitten shaped, terete or nearly so, semiglossy, variably colored (monochrome purple, tan, brown, or bichrome tan and purple), smooth, with punctiform hilum in notch. One-seeded indehiscent fruit, concealed by calyx and marcescent corolla, 2-2.7 x 1.3-2 x 1.2-1.7 mm, obovate, compressed to subterete, glossy and dull (upper one-third glossy and lower two-thirds dull), brown to tan, smooth.

Notes: Herbaceous short-lived perennial of Europe, naturalized in pastures and waste places throughout the United States and cultivated as a major pasture and hay crop. Two forms, a double cut known as medium red clover and single cut known as mammoth red clover, are available for planting.

Trifolium Linnaeus
Trifolieae, Faboideae

Species: *repens* Linnaeus.

Common Names: White clover, ladino clover.

Seed 0.9-1.2 x 0.8-1.1 x 0.8-1 mm, mitten shaped, subterete, dull, yellowish tan to brown, smooth, with punctiform hilum in notch. Three-seeded indehiscent fruit, concealed by calyx and marcescent corolla, 2.8-3 x 1.5-1.7 x 1 mm, oblong, subterete, semiglossy, tan, smooth.

Notes: Herbaceous perennial of Eurasia, naturalized in fields, lawns, and meadows and cultivated throughout the United States. Three main genotypes with similar seed are recognized: Small or wild; intermediate, common, or Dutch; and ladino or giant.

Trifolium Linnaeus
Trifolieae, Faboideae

Species: *resupinatum* Linnaeus.

Common Names: Persian clover, reversed clover.

Seed 1.4-2 x 1.4-1.5 x 1 mm, oblong to subcircular, terete or nearly so, semi-glossy, tan to purplish or yellowish tan or brown, smooth, with punctiform marginal hilum. One-seeded indehiscent fruit, concealed by calyx and marcescent corolla, 1.7-2.3 x 1.5-1.6 x 1.1 mm, oblong, terete or nearly so, dull, tan, smooth.

Notes: Herbaceous annual of Old World, naturalized in scattered pastures from Massachusetts to Wisconsin and South Dakota, south to Alabama, Oklahoma and Texas. Persian clover occasionally is cultivated in southeastern states.

Trifolium incarnatum 7.2X

Trifolium pratense 6.4X

Trifolium repens 8.0X

Trifolium resupinatum 9.6X

113

Trifolium Linnaeus
Trifolieae, Faboideae

Species: *subterraneum* Linnaeus.

Common Name: Subterranean clover.

Seed 2.3-3.2 x 2.2-2.6 x 2 mm, mitten shaped, terete or nearly so, glossy, dark reddish brown (some seeds nearly blackish or whitish), smooth, with punctiform hilum in notch. One-seeded indehiscent fruits (2-3 single indehiscent fruits surrounded by fibrous involucre and marescent corolla and maturing underground), 2.6-3.5 x 2.5-2.8 x 2.2 mm, elliptic, subterete, dull, tan, smooth.

Notes: Herbaceous annual grown in combination with other species for pasture in the Pacific Coast states and also cultivated to a limited extent in southeastern states.

Trigonella Linnaeus
Trifolieae, Faboideae

Species: *foenum-graceum* Linnaeus.

Common Name: Fenugreek.

Seed 3.5-5 x 2.5-3 x 2 mm, rectangular to trapeziform or oblong, compressed, smooth, dull, reddish tan to reddish brown, minutely tuberculate, with punctiform hilum in notch and concealed by whitish funicular remnant.

Notes: Herbaceous annual of Europe, grown to a limited extent as a winter green manure crop in California. Seeds have a distinct odor and are used for medicinal purposes in some countries.

Ulex Linnaeus
Genisteae, Faboideae

Species: *europaeus* Linnaeus.

Common names; Gorse, furze.

Seed 2.8-3.3 x 2.1-2.6 x 2 mm, mitten shaped, compressed to subterete, glossy, variously colored (brown, greenish tan, dark green, reddish brown), minutely tuberculate, with circular hilum in notch concealed by honey-colored aril.

Notes: Shrub of Europe, cultivated and naturalized in sandy soils and waste places along both east and west coasts (Massachusetts to Virginia and British Columbia to California). Gorse has become a serious weed on farm lands and burned or cutover timber areas and is a fire hazard because it burns readily when green.

Vicia Linnaeus
Vicieae, Faboideae

Species: *benghalensis* Linnaeus.

Common Name: Purple vetch.

Seed 3.7-5 x 3.7-4.5 x 3-3.5 mm, subcircular to oblong, compressed to subterete, dull (because of grayish bloom), gray with black mottles which may coalesce causing seeds to be blackish, smooth, with linear marginal hilum concealed by white funicular remnant.

Notes: Herbaceous annual of southern Europe, naturalized and cultivated as a cover and green manure or hay crop in the Pacific Coast states. Previously known as *Vicia atropurpurea* Desfontaines.

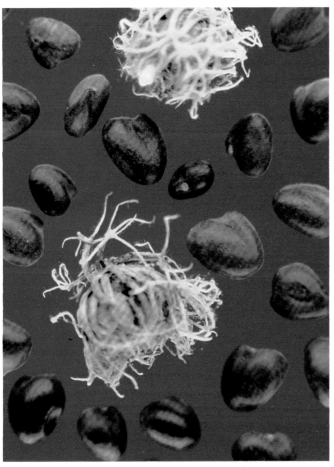

Trifolium subterraneum 5.6X

Trigonella foenum-graecum 4.8X

Ulex europaeus 7.2X

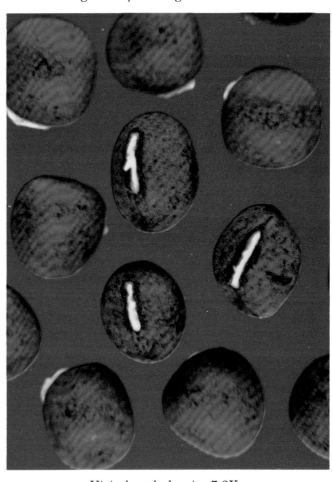

Vicia benghalensis 7.2X

Vicia Linnaeus
Vicieae, Faboideae

Species: *faba* Linnaeus.

Common Names: Broadbean, horsebean, windsorbean, pigeonbean, tickbean, sowbean.

Seed 7-30.5 x 6.5-17 x 4.5-9 mm, oblong to ovate, compressed, semiglossy, variously colored (brown, reddish brown, light to dark greenish brown, light to dark purple) occasionally obscurely mottled with colors similar to base colors, somewhat rugose or not, with elliptic to oblong hilum along end of seed and concealed or not by funicular remnant.

Notes: Herbaceous annual of Europe, cultivated for its edible seed in northern United States and escaping in California. Some people of southern European origin, who eat these seeds, may develop favism, a disease which manifests itself as acute haemolytic anemia.

Vicia Linnaeus
Vicieae, Faboideae

Species: *grandiflora* Scopoli var. *kitaibeliana* W. Koch.

Common Names: Showy vetch, bigflower vetch.

Seed 3-4.2 x 3-3.2 x 2-2.3 mm, circular, compressed, semiglossy, straw colored mottled or not with black which may coalesce causing seeds to be blackish, smooth, with linear hilum occupying 75% of seed circumference and concealed by whitish funicular remnant.

Notes: Herbaceous annual of Eurasia, naturalized from Delaware to Missouri, south to Florida and Mississippi.

Vicia Linnaeus
Vicieae, Faboideae

Species: *leavenworthii* Torrey & Gray.

Common Name: Mogollon vetch, Texas vetch.

Seed 1.9-3 x 1.9-3 x 2-2.5 mm, circular, terete, dull, greenish ochre to reddish brown mottled with darker brown, smooth, with wedge-shaped marginal hilum.

Notes: Herbaceous annual of Oklahoma and Texas and prevalent in the Edwards Plateau area.

Vicia Linnaeus
Vicieae, Faboideae

Species: *nigricans* Hooker & Arnott subsp. *gigantea* (Hooker & Arnott) Lassetter & Gunn.

Common Name: Large vetch.

Seed 5.5-6.3 x 5.5-6.3 x 4.5-5.2 mm, circular, terete, dull, ochre to reddish ochre usually moderately to densely mottled with darker brown making seeds appear to be monochrome dark brown, smooth, with linear hilum occupying 75% of seed circumference.

Notes: Herbaceous perennial vine of coastal areas and stream banks from Alaska to California. Known in U.S. floras as *Vicia gigantea* Hooker & Arnott.

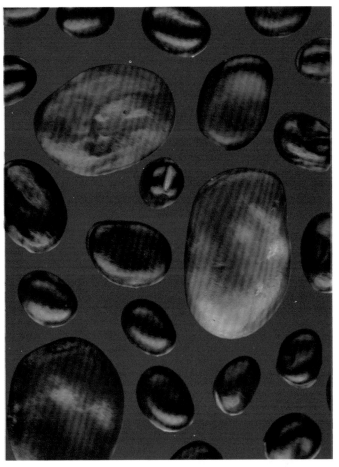

Vicia faba 2.4X

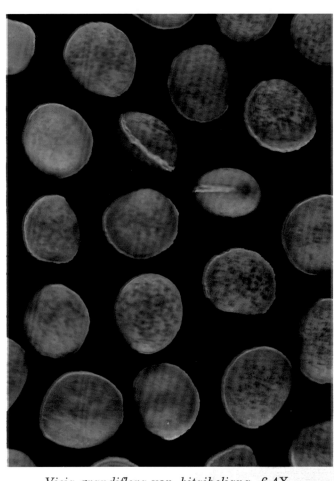

Vicia grandiflora var. *kitaibeliana* 6.4X

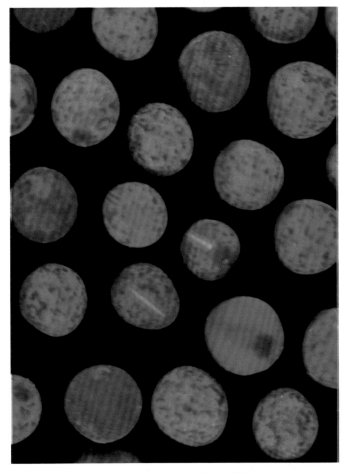

Vicia leavenworthii 9.6X

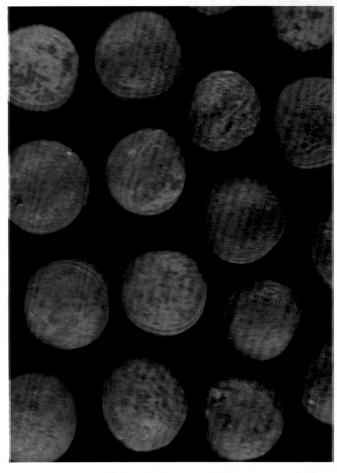

Vicia nigricans 4.8X

117

Vicia Linnaeus
Vicieae, Faboideae

Species: *pannonica* Crantz.

Common Name: Showy vetch, Hungarian vetch.

Seed 3.5-4.5 x 3.5-x 4 x 3-3.3 mm, subtriangular to subcircular, terete or nearly so, dull, rosy brown mottled with brown and black, smooth, with oblong marginal hilum partially concealed or not by whitish funicular remnant.

Notes: Herbaceous annual of Europe, naturalized in Sonona County, California and cultivated in Oregon and Washington for pasture, green manure, and silage.

Vicia Linnaeus
Vicieae, Faboideae

Species: *sativa* Linnaeus subsp. *nigra* (Linnaeus) Ehrhart.

Common Names: Blackpod vetch, narrow-leaved vetch, wild vetch.

Seed 2.3-4 x 2.3-4 x 2.3-4 mm, circular, terete, dull, variously colored (monochrome velvety black, buff, reddish brown, or greenish buff to reddish buff mottled with dark brown), smooth, with wedge-shaped marginal hilum.

Notes: Herbaceous annual of Eurasia, naturalized in waste places, roadsides, and fields from Nova Scotia to Michigan and Minnesota, south to Florida, Missouri, Oklahoma, Texas as well as Idaho and California. Known in some U.S. floras as *Vicia angustifolia* Reichard.

Vicia Linnaeus
Vicieae, Faboideae

Species: *sativa* Linnaeus subsp. *sativa*.

Common Names: Common vetch, spring vetch.

Seed 4.5-6 x 4.5-6 x 2.7-5 mm, circular-rectangular (pillow-shaped) to circular or ovate, compressed to nearly terete, dull, variously colored (pale buff to dark greenish ochre or green and mottled with tan to brown and with mottles coalescing causing seeds to be dark brown to nearly blackish), smooth, with wedge-shaped marginal hilum.

Notes: Herbaceous annual of Europe, naturalized in waste places, roadsides and fields from Virginia to Alabama and Texas and California to Washington. Common vetch is cultivated in Oregon and Washington for green manure, hay, pasture, and seed, and used for green manure in southeastern states.

Vicia Linnaeus
Vicieae, Faboideae

Species: *villosa* Roth subsp. *varia* (Host) Corbiere.

Common Names: Winter vetch, woolypod vetch.

Seed 3.2-4.7 x 3.2-4 x 3-3.5 mm, circular to oblong, terete, dull, reddish brown to grayish brown obscurely mottled with darker brown, smooth, with oblong to slightly wedge-shaped marginal hilum.

Notes: Herbaceous annual of Europe, naturalized along roadsides, in waste places and fields, from Virginia to Florida, west to Kentucky and Mississippi as well as Texas and California. Winter vetch is cultivated for green manure and forage in the southeastern states and is often known as *Vicia dasycarpa* Tenore in U.S. floras.

118

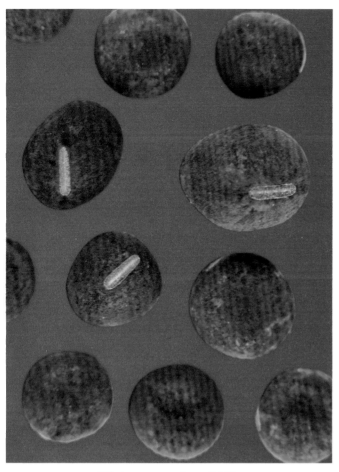

Vicia pannonica   7.2X

Vicia sativa subsp. *nigra*   2.8X

Vicia sativa subsp. *sativa*   4.0X

Vicia villosa subsp. *varia*   7.2X

Vicia Linnaeus
Vicieae, Faboideae

Species: *villosa* Roth subsp. *villosa.*

Common Name: Hairy vetch.

Seed 2.7-4.9 x 2.3-4.9 x 2-3.8 mm, circular, subterete to terete, dull, dark reddish brown to dull greenish brown mottled with blackish brown, smooth, with oblong marginal hilum.

Notes: Herbaceous annual to weak perennial of Europe, naturalized along roadsides and in waste places, and fields from Nova Scotia to British Columbia, south to Georgia, Texas and California. Hairy vetch is cultivated for green manure and for forage in combination with small grains.

Vigna Savi
Phaseolinae, Phaseoleae, Faboideae

Species: *angularis* (Willdenow) Ohwi & Ohashi.

Common Name: Adzuki-bean.

Seed 5-7.5 x 4-6 x 3-5 mm, oblong, subterete, semiglossy to dull, variably colored (monochrome tan, greenish tan, purple or tan, reddish brown, greenish tan mottled with black), smooth, with linear marginal hilum concealed by whitish funicular remnant.

Notes: Herbaceous annual, occasionally cultivated in home gardens for its edible seeds. Previously known as *Phaseolus angularis* (Willdenow) F. W. Wight.

Vigna Savi
Phaseolinae, Phaseoleae, Faboideae

Species: *radiata* (Linnaeus) Wilczek.

Common Name: Mung-bean, chickasaw-pea, Oregon-pea, Neuman-pea, Newman-bean, chopsuey-bean.

Seed 3.3-4.8 x 3-3.5 x 3-4 mm, rectangular, terete, glossy to dull, variably colored (monochrome tan, greenish tan, purple or greenish to reddish brown mottled with black), smooth to minutely tuberculate or reticulate, with oblong marginal hilum concealed by whitish funicular remnant.

Notes: Herbaceous annual of southern Asia, cultivated in United States for bean sprouts. Mung-bean was previously known as *Phaseolus aureus* Roxburgh.

Vigna Savi
Phaseolinae, Phaseoleae, Faboideae

Species: *unguiculata* (Linnaeus) Walpers subsp. *sesquipedalis* (Linnaeus) Verdcourt.

Common Names: Asparagus-bean, yardlong-bean.

Seed 8-12 x 4-6 x 3-4 mm, oblong, compressed, dull, variably colored (monochrome tan, purple, black or bicolored ivory and reddish brown or brown or one of the base colors streaked with darker colored), faintly rugose or not, with wedge shaped marginal hilum concealed by whitish funicular remnant and except black seeds, surrounded by black eye.

Notes: Herbaceous annual of central Africa, cultivated as far north as southern Illinois, Ohio, and New Jersey. Asparagus-bean is lower yielding than southern-pea (subsp. *unguiculata*) and not as palatable as beans (*Phaseolus* spp.). Previously known as *Vigna sinensis* (Linnaeus) Savi ex Hasskarl subsp. *sesquipedalis* (Linnaeus) van Eseltine.

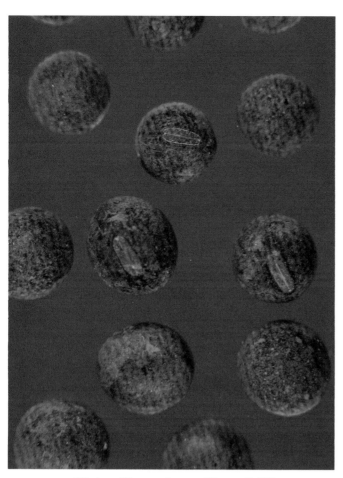

Vicia villosa subsp. *villosa*   7.2X

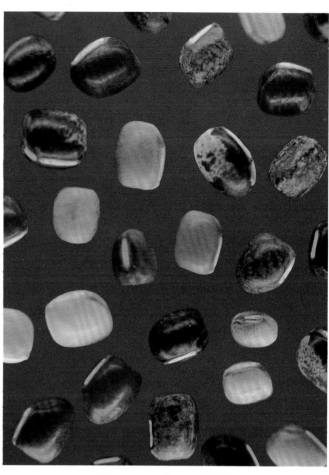

Vigna angularis   3.2X

Vigna radiata   5.6X

Vigna unguiculata subsp. *sesquipedalis*   2.8X

Vigna Savi
Phaseolinae, Phaseoleae, Faboideae
Species: *unguiculata* (Linnaeus) Walpers subsp. *unguiculata.*
Common Names: Southern-pea, cream-pea, cowpea, blackeyed-pea.
Seed 4.5-10 x 4.5-6.5 x 3-6 mm, oblong or nearly so, compressed, dull, variably colored (monochrome ivory, tan, reddish brown, purple, black or bichrome ivory and black or black mottled with reddish brown), rugose or not, with wedge-shaped marginal hilum concealed by whitish funicular remnant.
Notes: Herbaceous annual of central Africa, adapted to the same area as subsp. *sesquipedalis.* Widely cultivated for forage, green manure, and edible seeds which are consumed as green pods or shelled seeds. Previously known as *Vigna sinensis* (Linnaeus) Endlicher.

Wisteria Nuttall
Millettieae, Faboideae
Species: *frutescens* (Linnaeus) Poiret.
Common Name: Wisteria.
Seed 10-11 x 7-8 x 7-8 mm, oblong, terete, glossy, dark reddish brown, smooth, with oblong marginal hilum concealed by whitish funicular remnant.
Notes: Woody vine of moist or wet woods and river banks, from Virginia to Florida, west to Arkansas and Texas. Two varieties are recognized in United States: var. *frutescens* and var. *macrostachya* (Nuttall) Torrey & Gray.

Wisteria Nuttall
Millettieae, Faboideae
Species: *sinensis* (Sims) Sweet.
Common Names: Chinese wisteria, purple wisteria vine.
Seed 13-17 x 12-18 x 4 mm, subcircular to suboblong, flattened, glossy, dark reddish brown mottled with black, somewhat rugose, with oblong marginal hilum concealed by whitish funicular remnant and with tongue-aril.
Notes: Woody vine or shrub of Asia, cultivated and naturalized in open woods and road-sides from Virginia to Florida, west to Tennessee and Mississippi. Ingested seeds are poisonous to humans.

Zornia J. F. Gmelin
Aeschynomeneae, Faboideae
Species: *bracteata* (Walter) J. F. Gmelin.
Common Name: Zornia.
Seed: 2.2-2.4 x 1.4-1.6 x 0.8 mm, falcate, compressed, semiglossy, reddish brown to tan rarely mottled with purple, smooth, with punctiform marginal hilum with a darker reddish brown or tannish eye. Loment 3.5-4 x 2.5-3 x 1.2 mm (excluding spines), D-shaped and truncate at each end of apical section with curved style or if basal section with stipe, compressed, dull, tan, reticulate and spiny.
Notes: Herbaceous perennial of dry sandy woods and openings from Virginia south to Florida and Texas.

Vigna unguiculata subsp. *unguiculata* 2.8X

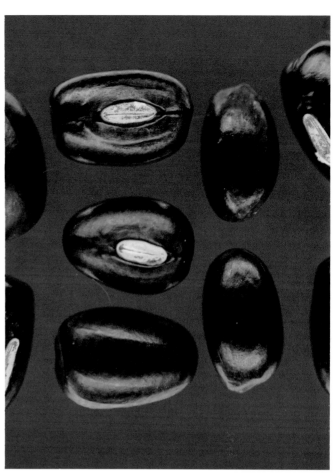

Wisteria frutescens 3.2X

Wisteria sinensis 3.2X

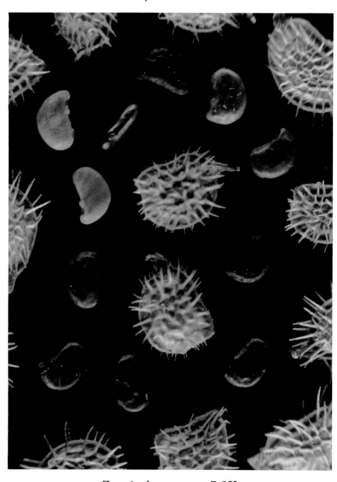

Zornia bracteata 7.2X

Literature Cited

Barkley, T. M. 1977. *Atlas of the Flora of the Great Plains.* 600 pp. Iowa State University Press, Ames.

Barneby, R. C. 1964. *Atlas of North American Astragalus.* Parts 1 and 2. New York Bot. Gard. Mem. 13: 1-1188.

Barneby, R. C. 1977. *Daleae Imagines.* New York Bot. Gard. Mem. 27: 1-891.

Boelcke, O. 1946. *Estudio Morfologico de las Semillas de Leguminosas, Mimosoideas, y Caesalpinioideas de enteras Agronomico en la Argentina.* Darwiniana 7: 240-321.

Capitaine, L. 1912. *Les Graines de Legumineuses.* 459 pp. Emile Larose, Paris.

Corner, E. J. H. 1976. *The Seeds of Dicotyledons,* v. 1, 2. Cambridge University Press, Cambridge, England.

Correll, D. S. and M. C. Johnston. 1970. *Manual of the Vascular Plants of Texas.* 1881 pp. Texas Research Foundation, Renner.

Delorit, R. J. 1970. *An Illustrated Taxonomy Manual of Weed Seeds.* 175 pp. Agronomy Publications, River Falls.

Duke, J. A. 1981. *Handbook of Legumes of World Economic Importance.* 345 pp. Plenum, New York.

Fernald, M. L. 1950. *Gray's Manual of Botany,* ed. 8. 1632 pp. American Book Co., New York.

Gleason, H. A. 1952. *The New Britton and Brown Illustrated Flora of the Northeastern United States and Adjacent Canada.* Vol. 2, pp. 379-453. The New York Botanical Garden, Bronx.

Gunn, C. R. 1969. *Abrus precatorius: A Deadly Gift.* Garden Journal, Jan-Feb: 2-5.

Gunn, C. R. 1981a. *Seed Topography in the Fabaceae.* Seed Sci. & Tech. 9: 737-757.

Gunn, C. R. 1981b. *Seeds of Leguminosae.* In R. M. Polhill and P. H. Raven, eds., *Advances in Legume Systematics,* pt. 2, pp. 913-925. Internatl. Legume Conf., Kew, Proc. 1978, v. 2. Min. Agr., Fisheries and Food, Richmond, England.

Gunn, C. R. 1983 *A nomenclator of Legume (Fabaceae) Genera.* 224 pp. U.S. Dept. Agr. Tech. Bull. 1680. Government Printing Office, Washington, D.C.

Gunn, C. R., Chairman, W. H. Cross, D. R. Dewey, P. A. Fryxell, A. M. Golden, R. E. Hanneman, Jr., G. B. Hewitt, P. L. Lentz, J. R. Lichtenfels, F. G. Meyer, D. R. Miller, F. D. Parker, and T. G. Pridham. 1977. *Systematic Collections of the Agricultural Research Service.* U.S. Dept. Agr. Misc. Pub. 1343. Government Printing Office, Washington, D.C.

Gunn, C. R., J. V. Dennis, and P. J. Paradine. 1976. *World Guide to Tropical Drift Seeds and Fruits.* 240 pp. Quadrangle/The New York Times Book Co., New York.

Gunn, C. R., W. H. Skrdla, and H. C. Spencer. 1978. *Classification of Medicago sativa L. Using Legume Characters and Flower Colors.* 84 pp. U.S. Dept. of Agr. Tech. Bull. 1574. Government Printing Office, Washington, D.C.

Hitchcock, C. L., A. Cronquist, M. Ownbey, and J. W. Thompson. 1961. *Vascular Plants of the Pacific Northwest.* Part 3, 614 pp. University of Washington Press, Seattle.

Hulten, Eric. 1968. *Flora of Alaska and Neighboring Territories.* 1008 pp. Stanford University Press, Stanford, California.

Irwin, H. S. and R. C. Barneby. 1982. *The American Cassiinae.* New York Bot. Gard. Mem. 35(1-2): 1-918.

Isely, D. 1955. *Observations on Seeds of the Leguminosae: Mimosoideae and Caesalpinioideae.* Iowa Acad. Sci. Proc. 62: 142-148.

Isely, D. 1973. *Leguminosae of the United States: I. Subfamily Mimosoideae.* New York Bot. Gard. Mem. 25(1): 1-152.

Isely, D. 1975. *Leguminosae of the United States: II. Subfamily Caesalpinioideae.* New York Bot. Gard. Mem. 25(2): 1-228.

Isely, D. 1981. *Leguminosae of the United States: III. Subfamily Papilionoideae:* Tribes *Sophoreae, Podalyrieae, Loteae.* New York Bot. Gard. Mem. 29(3): 1-264.

Isely, D. 1982. *Leguminosae and Homo sapiens.* Econ. Bot. 36: 46-70.

Isley, D. and R. M. Polhill. 1980. *Leguminosae Subfamily Papilionoideae.* Taxon 29: 105-119.

Kartesz, J. T. and R. Kartesz. 1980. *A Synonymized Checklist of the Vascular Flora of the United States, Canada, and Greenland.* 497 pp. University of North Carolina Press, Chapel Hill.

Kearney, T. H. and R. H. Peebles. 1951. *Arizona Flora.* 1032 pp. University of California Press, Berkeley.

Lersten, N. R. 1981. *Testa Topography in Leguminosae, subfamily Papilionoideae.* Iowa Acad. Sci., Proc. 88 (4): 180-191.

Lersten, N. R. and C. R. Gunn. 1982. *Testa Characters in Tribe Vicieae, with Notes about Tribes Abreae, Cicereae, and Trifolieae (Fabaceae).* 40 pp. U.S. Dept. Agr. Tech. Bull. 1667. Government Printing Office, Washington, D.C.

Long, R. W. and O. Lakela. 1971. *A Flora of Tropical Florida.* 962 pp. University of Miami Press, Coral Gables.

Munz, P. A. and D. D. Keck. 1959. *California Flora.* 1681 pp. University of California Press, Berkeley.

National Academy of Sciences. 1979. *Tropical Legumes: Resources of the Future.* 328 pp. National Academy of Sciences, Washington, D.C.

Ohashi, H. 1978. *The Taxonomy and Distribution of Euchresta japonica (Leguminosae).* Bot. Mag. Tokyo 91: 291-294.

Polhill, R. M. 1982. *Crotalaria in Africa and Madagascar.* 389 pp. A. A. Balkema, Rotterdam.

Polhill, R. M. and P. H. Raven. 1981. *Advances in Legume Systematics,* pt. 1, pp. 1-425 + index. Internatl. Legume Conf., Kew, Proc. 1978, v. 2. Min. Agr., Fisheries and Food, Richmond, England.

Radford, A. E., H. E. Ahles, and C. R. Bell. 1968. *Manual of the Vascular Flora of the Carolinas.* 1183 pp. University of North Carolina Press, Chapel Hill.

Rugenstein, S. R. and N. R. Lersten. 1981. *Stomata on seeds and fruits of Bauhinia (Leguminosae: Caesalpinioidieae).* Amer. Jour. Bot. 68: 873-876.

Scoggan, H. J. 1978. *The Flora of Canada,* part 3, pp. 968-1035. Nat. Mus. Nat. Sci. Pub. in Bot. No. 7 (3), Ottawa.

Skerman, P. J. 1977. *Tropical Forage Legumes.* Food and Agriculture Organization United Nations Plant Product and Protection Series No. 2, pp. 1-632.

Soil Conservation Service. 1982. *National List of Scientific Plant Names:* Volume 1, List of Plant Names. 416 pp. U.S. Dept. Agr. SCS-TP-159. Government Printing Office, Washington, D.C.

Steyermark, J. A. 1963. *Flora of Missouri.* 1725 pp. Iowa State University Press, Ames.

Summerfield, R. J. and A. H. Bunting. 1980. *Advances in Legume Science.* Internatl. Legume Conf., Kew, Proc. 1978. v. 1, pp. 1-667. Min. Agr., Fisheries and Food, Richmond, England.

Voss, E. G., H. M. Burdet, W. G. Chaloner, V. Demoulin, W. Greuter, P. Hiepko, J. McNeill, R. D. Meikle, D. H. Nicolson, R. C. Rollins, and P. C. Silva. 1983. *International code of Botanical Nomenclature.* 472 pp. Bohn, Scheltema and Holkema, Utrecht, Netherlands.

Appendix I: Phylogenetic List of Studied Species

CAESALPINIOIDEAE

Caesalpinieae
Gymnocladus dioica (Linnaeus) Koch
Gleditsia aquatica Marshall
Gleditsia triacanthos Linnaeus
Peltophorum pterocarpum (A. P. de candolle) Backer ex K. Heyne
Delonix regia (Bojer ex Hooker) Rafinesque
Caesalpinia bonduc (Linnaeus) Roxburgh
Caesalpinia coriacea (Jacquin) Willdenow
Caesalpinia gilliesii (Wallich ex W. J. Hooker) A. Dietrich
Caesalpinia pulcherrima (Linnaeus) Swartz
Caesalpinia sappan Linnaeus
Hoffmannseggia glauca (Ortega) Eifert
Haematoxylum campechianum Linnaeus
Parkinsonia aculeata Linnaeus

Cassieae
Ceratonia siliqua Linnaeus
Cassia fistula Linnaeus
Cassia javanica Linnaeus
Senna alata (Linnaeus) Rosburgh
Senna didymobotrya (Fresenius) Irwin & Barneby
Senna occidentalis (Linnaeus) Irwin & Barneby
Chamaecrista absus Linnaeus
Chamaecrista fasciculata (Michaux) Greene
Chamaecrista nictitans (Linnaeus) Moench

Cercideae
Cercis canadensis Linnaeus
Bauhinia monarda Kurz
Bauhinia tomentosa Linnaeus

Detarieae
Afzelia quanzensis Welwitsch
Hymenaea courbaril Linnaeus

Amherstieae
Tamarindus indica Linnaeus

MIMOSOIDEAE

Parkieae
Parkia javanica Merrill

Mimozygantheae
Mimozyganthus carinatus (Grisebach) Burkart

Mimoseae
Adenanthera pavonina Linnaeus
Prosopis glandulosa Torrey
Entada gigas (Linnaeus) Fawcett & Rendle
Mimosa borealis A. Gray
Mimosa dysocarpa Bentham
Mimosa pigra Linnaeus var. *berlandieri* (A. Gray) B. L. Turner

Schrankia uncinata Willdenow
Leucaena leucocephala (Lamarck) de Wit
Dichrostachys cinerea (Linnaeus) Wight & Arnott
Desmanthus illinoensis (Michaux) Macmillian ex Robinson & Fernald
Desmanthus leptolobus Torrey & Gray
Neptunia pubescens Bentham

Acacieae
Acacia angustissima (P. Miller) O. Kuntze var. *hirta* (Nuttall) B. L. Robinson
Acacia cyclops A. Cunningham ex G. Don
Acacia decurrens (Wendland) Willdenow
Acacia farnesiana (Linnaeus) Willdenow
Acacia toruosa (Linnaeus) Willdenow

Ingeae
Albizia julibrissin Durazzini
Albizia lebbeck (Linnaeus) Bentham
Lysiloma sabicu Bentham
Enterolobium cyclocarpum (Jacquin) Grisebach
Calliandra eriophylla Bentham
Calliandra humilis Bentham
Pithecellobium dulce (Roxburgh) Bentham

FABOIDEAE

Swartzieae
Swartzia simplex (Swartz) Sprengel

Sophoreae
Maackia amurensis Ruprecht
Cladastris lutea (Michaux) Koch
Sophora tomentosa Linnaeus

Dipteryxeae
Dipteryx odorata (Aublet) Willdenow

Dalbergieae
Andira inermis (W. Wright) Kunth
Dalbergia sissoo Roxburg ex de Candolle

Abreae
Abrus precatorius Linnaeus

Millettieae
Lonchocarpus violaceus Kunth
Piscidia piscipula (Linnaeus) Sargent
Pongamia pinnata (Linnaeus) Merrill
Tephrosia virginiana (Linnaeus) Persoon
Wisteria frutescens (Linnaeus) Poiret
Wisteria sinensis (Sims) Sweet

Robineae
Robinia pseudoaccacia Linnaeus
Olneya tesota A. Gray
Coursetia microphylla A. Gray
Cracca edwardsii A. Gray
Peteria thompsonae S. Watson

126

Sphinctospermum constrictum (S. Watson) Rose
Genistidium dumosum I. M. Johnston
Diphysa thurberi (A. Gray) Rydberg
Sesbania macrocarpa Muhlenberg ex Rafinesque
Glottidium vesicaria (Jacquin) C. Mohr

Indigofereae
Indigofera hirsuta Linnaeus
Cyamopsis tetragonoloba (Linnaeus) Taubert

Desmodieae
Desmodium canadense (Linnaeus) de Candolle
Desmodium glutinosum (Muhlenberg) Wood
Desmodium tortuosum (Swartz) de Candolle
Alysicarpus vaginalis (Linnaeus) de Candolle
Lespedeza cuneata (Dumont de Courset) G. Don
Lespedeza stipulacea Maximowicz
Lespedeza striata (Thunberg) Hooker & Arnott
Lespedeza virginica (Linnaeus) Britton

Phaseoleae
Erythrininae
Erythrina crista-galli Linnaeus
Erythrina herbacea Linnaeus
Mucuna deeringiana (Bortero) Merrill
Mucuna pruriens (Linnaeus) de Candolle
Mucuna sloanei Fawcett & Rendle
Apios americana Medikus
Diocleinae
Dioclea multiflora (Torrey & Gray) C. Mohr
Dioclea reflexa Hooker f.
Canavalia ensiformis (Linnaeus) de Candolle
Pachyrrhizus erosus (Linnaeus) Urban
Galactia volubilis (Linnaeus) Britton
Glycininae
Pueraria lobata (Willdenow) Ohwi
Glycine max (Linnaeus) Merrill
Cologania angustifolia Kunth
Amphicarpaea bracteata (Linnaeus) Fernald
Ophrestiinae
Ophrestia radicosa (A. Richards) Verdcourt
Kennediinae
Kennedia rubicunda Ventenat
Clitoriinae
Centrosema virginiana (Linnaeus) Bentham
Clitoria ternatea Linnaeus
Phaseolinae
Lablab purpureus Linnaeus
Vigna angularis (Willdenow) Ohwi & Ohashi
Vigna radiata (Linnaeus) Wilczek
Vigna unguiculata (Linnaeus) Walpers subsp.
sesquipedalis (Linnaeus) Verdcourt
Vigna unguiculata (Linnaeus) Walpers
subsp. *unguiculata*
Strophostyles helvola (Linnaeus) Elliott
Macroptilium lathyroides (Linnaeus) Urban

Phaseolus coccineus Linnaeus
Phaseolus lunatus Linnaeus
Phaseolus vulgaris Linnaeus
Cajaninae
Cajanus cajan (Linnaeus) Huth
Rhynchosia minima (Linnaeus) de Candolle

Psoraleeae
Psoralea bituminosa Linnaeus
Psoralea orbicularis Lindley
Orbexilum pedunculatum Rydberg

Amorpheae
Eysenhardtia texana Scheele
Parryella filifolia Torrey & Gray
Amorpha canescens Pursh
Amorpha fruticosa Linnaeus
Errazurizia rotunda (Wooton) Barneby
Psorothamnus arborescens (Torrey) Barneby var.
minutifolius (Parish) Barneby
Psorothamnus scoparius (A. Gray) Rydberg
Marina parryi (Torrey & Gray) Barneby
Dalea leporina (Aiton) A. A. Bullock
Dalea purpurea Ventenat

Aeschynomeneae
Nissolia schottii (Torrey) A. Gray
Aeschynomene indica Linnaeus
Zornia bracteata (Walter) J. F. Gmelin
Chapmannia floridana Torrey & Gray
Stylosanthes biflora (Linnaeus) Britton, Sterns,
Poggenberg
Arachis hypogaea Linnaeus

Adesmieae
Adesmia incana Vogel

Galegeae
Colutea arborescens Linnaeus
Sphaerophysa salsula (Pallas) de Candolle
Caragana arborescens Lamarck
Astragalus canadensis Linnaeus
Astragalus crassicarpus Nuttall var. *crassicarpus*
Astragalus drummondii Douglas ex Hooker
Astragalus purshii Douglas ex Hooker
Oxytropis campestris (Linnaeus) de Candolle
Oxytropis sericea Nuttall
Alhagi maurorum Medikus subsp. *maurorum*
Galega officinalis Linnaeus
Glycyrrhiza lepidota (Nuttall) Pursh

Carmichaelieae
Carmichaelia arenaria G. Simpson

Hedysareae
Hedysarum alpinum Linnaeus var. *americanum*
Michaux
Onobrychis viciifolia Scopoli

127

Loteae

Anthyllis vulneraria Linnaeus
Lotus corniculata Linnaeus
Lotus purshianus (Bentham) Clements & Clements
Lotus uliginosus Schkuhr

Coronilleae

Coronilla varia Linnaeus
Scorpiurus muricatus Linnaeus
Ornithopus sativus Brotero

Vicieae

Vicia benghalensis Linnaeus
Vicia faba Linnaeus
Vicia grandiflora Scopoli var. *kitaibeliana* Koch
Vicia leavenworthii Torrey & Gray
Vicia nigricans Hooker & Arnott subsp. *gigantea*
    (Hooker & Arnott) Lassetter & Gunn
Vicia pannonica Crantz
Vicia sativa Linnaeus subsp. *nigra* (Linnaeus) Ehrhart
Vicia sativa Linnaeus subsp. *sativa*
Vicia villosa Roth subsp. *varia* (Host) Corbiere
Vicia villosa Roth subsp. *villosa*
Lathyrus hirsutus Linnaeus
Lathyrus latifolius Linnaeus
Lathyrus odoratus Linnaeus
Lathyrus sylvestris Linnaeus
Lens culinaris Medikus
Pisum sativum Linnaeus

Cicereae

Cicer arietinum Linnaeus

Trifolieae

Ononis spinosa Linnaeus
Melilotus alba Medikus
Melilotus indica (Linnaeus) Allioni
Melilotus officinalis Lamarck
Trigonella foenum-graceum Linnaeus
Medicago arabica (Linnaeus) Hudson
Medicago lupulina Linnaeus
Medicago orbicularis (Linnaeus) Bartalini
Medicago polymorpha Linnaeus
Medicago sativa Linnaeus
Trifolium arvense Linnaeus
Trifolium dubium Sibthorp

Trifolium fragiferum Linnaeus
Trifolium hirtum Allioni
Trifolium hybridum Linnaaeus
Trifolium incarnatum Linnaeus
Trifolium pratense Linnaeus
Trifolium repens Linnaeus
Trifolium resupinatum Linnaeus
Trifolium subterraneum Linnaeus

Brongniartieae

Brongniartia minutiflora S. Watson

Mirbelieae

Daviesia horrida Meissner

Bossiaeeae

Bossiaea heterophylla Ventenat

Podalyrieae

Podalyria calyptrata (Retzius) Willldenow

Liparieae

Hypocalyptus sophorides (Bergius) Baillon

Crotalarieae

Crotalaria pallida Aiton
Crotalaria sagittalis Linnaeus
Crotalaria spectabilis Roth

Euchresteae

Euchrestia japonica Hooker f. ex Regel

Thermopsideae

Thermopsis villosa (Walter) Fernald & Schubert
Baptisia australis (Linnaeus) R. Brown
Pickeringia montana Nuttall ex Torrey & Gray
    var. *tomentosa* (Abrams) I. M. Johnston

Genisteae

Lupinus albus Linnaeus
Lupinus angustifolius Linnaeus
Lupinus chamissonis Eschscholtz
Lupinus leucophyllus Douglas ex Lindley
Lupinus polyphyllus Lindley
Laburnum anagyroides Medikus
Cytisus scoparius (Linnaeus) Link
Spartium junceum Linnaeus
Genista tinctoria Linnaeus
Ulex europaeus Linnaeus

Appendix II: Genera Included in this book of Tribes and Subtribes of Phaseoleae Not Present in Continental United States.

Adesmia (Adesmieae)
Afzelia (Detarieae)
Bossiaea (Bossiaeeae)
Carmichaelia (Carmichaelieae)
Dipteryx (Dipteryxeae)
Euchresta (Euchresteae)
Hymenaea (Detarieae)

Hypocalyptus (Liparieae)
Kennedia (Kennediinae, Phaseoleae)
Mimozyganthus (Mimozygantheae)
Ophrestia (Ophrestiinae, Phaseoleae)
Parkia (Parkieae)
Podalyria (Podalyrieae)
Swartzia (Swartzieae)

Index of Tribe Names

Index of Common Names

Lupine, western, 74,75
Lupine, white, 72,73
Luzerne, 78,79

Maackia, 76,77
Mammoth red clover, 112,113
Marina, parry, 76,77
Medick, black, 78,79
Medick, hop, 78,79
Medick, spotted, 76,77
Medium red clover, 112,113
Melilot, white, 80,81
Mesquite, 96,97
Mesquittella, 32,33
Mexican palo verde, 90,91
Milk-pea, 56,57
Milk-vetch, Canada, 24,25
Milk-vetch, drummond, 24,25
Milk-vetch, pursh, 26,27
Mimosa, 18,19,80,81,82,83
Mimosa, Texas, 82,83
Mimozyganthus, 82,83
Mock-mesquite, 32,33
Mogollon vetch, 116,117
Moneywort, false, 22,23
Mung-bean, 120,121

Narrow-leaved vetch, 118,119
Necklace pod, 104,105
Newman-bean, 120,121
Neuman-pea, 120,121
Nickernut, gray, 28,29
Nissolia, 84,85
No-eye-pea, 30,31
Nonesuch, 78,79

Old-field clover, 108,109
Ophrestia, 86,87
Orchid tree, pink, 26,27
Oregon-pea, 120,121
Overlook-bean, 32,33

Palo de hierra, 86,87
Parkia, 90,91
Parry marina, 76,77
Pea, English, 94,95
Pea, field, 94,95
Pea, garden, 94,95
Peanut, 24,25
Pearson-bean, 32,33
Peashrub, Siberian, 32,33
Peatree, caragana, 32,33
Peavine, 106,107
Pencil flower, 106,107
Perennial-pea, 66,67
Perennial sweet-pea, 66,67
Persian clover, 112,113
Peteria, 92,93
Pigeonbean, 116,117
Pigeon-pea, 30,31
Pignut, 62,63
Pindar, 24,25

Pink orchidtree, 26,27
Pink shower, 34,35
Pod, bladder, 58,59
Pod, necklace, 104,105
Podalyria, 96,97
Poinciana, 30,31
Poinciana, royal, 46,47
Pole bean, 94,95
Pomme de prairie, 24,25
Pongam, 96,97
Popinac, 70,71
Potatobean, American, 22,23
Prairie acacia, 14,15
Prairie-clover, purple, 46,47
Prairie-mimosa, 48,49
Prairie trefoil, 72,73
Precatory-bean, 14,15
Prickleweed, 48,49
Psoralea, 98,99
Psorothamnus, 98,99
Purple lonchocarpus, 70,71
Purple prairie-clover, 46,47
Purple vetch, 114,115
Purple wisteria vine, 122,123
Purse, sea, 50,51
Pursh milk-vetch, 26,27
Pussies, 108,109

Rabbit-pea, 108,109
Rabbitfoot clover, 108,109
Rattlebox, 42,43
Rattleweed, Canadian, 24,25
Redbud, 36,37
Red clover, 112,113
Red clover, mammoth, 112,113
Red clover, medium, 112,113
Red-gram, 30,31
Red sandlewood, 16,17
Restharrow, 86,87
Retama, 90,91
Reversed clover, 112,113
River-hemp, Colorado, 104,105
Rosary-pea, 14,15
Rose clover, 110,111
Rough-pea, 66,67
Royal poinciana, 46,47
Runner bean, 92,93
Runner bean, scarlet, 92,93
Rushpea, 62,63

Sainfoin, 86,87
Sandlewood, red, 16,17
St. John's bread, 36,37
Sampson snakeroot, 88,89
Sappanwood, 30,31
Scarlet runner bean, 92,93
Scorpiurus, 102,103
Scotch broom, 44,45
Seabean, 84,85
Sea heart, 52,53
Sea purse, 50,51

Seibo, 54,55
Senna, 102,103
Sensitive brier, 100,101
Sericea lespedeza, 68,69
Serradela, 88,89
Sesbania, 104,105
Shoestring, devil's, 60,61,108,109
Shoestrings, 20,21
Shower, golden, 34,35
Shower, pink, 34,35
Showy crotalaria, 44,45
Showy vetch, 116,117,118,119
Shrub, smoke, 98,99
Shuck, honey, 58,59
Siberian peashrub, 32,33
Silktree, 18,19
Singletary-pea, 66,67
Siratro, annual, 76,77
Slender lespedeza, 70,71
Small false-mesquite, 32,33
Small hop clover, 110,111
Small-leaved snoutbean, 100,101
Smoke shrub, 98,99
Smooth crotalaria, 42,43
Snakeroot, sampson, 88,89
Snoutbean, small-leaved, 100,101
Sourclover, 80,81
Southern burclover, 76,77
Southern-pea, 122,123
Sowbean, 116,117
Soybean, 60,61
Spanish-broom, 104,105
Sphinctospermum, 106,107
Spotted burclover, 76,77
Spotted medick, 76,77
Spring vetch, 118,119
Spurred butterfly-pea, 34,35
Sticktight, 48,49
Stone clover, 108,109
Strawberry clover, 110,111
Striate lespedeza, 68,69
Striped crotalaria, 42,43
Stypticweed, 102,103
Subterranean clover, 114,115
Swartzia, 106,107
Swedish clover, 110,111
Sweet acacia, 16,17
Sweetclover, annual yellow, 80,81
Sweetclover, white, 80,81
Sweetclover, annual yellow, 80,81
Sweetclover, yellow, 80,81
Sweet-pea, 66,67
Sweet-pea, common, 66,67
Sweet-pea, perennial, 66,67
Sweet root, 60,61
Sweet-vetch, 62,63

Tall indigo, 104,105
Tamarind, 96,97,108,109
Tesota, 86,87

Index of Scientific Names